UNIVERSITY OF NORTH CAROLINA

Studies in the Romance Languages and Literatures

NUMBER 31

I0660977

THE PEREGRINE MUSE

MICHELANGELO'S SKETCH OF BRONZE DAVID WITH STUDY OF RIGHT ARM OF MARBLE
DAVID AND SCHOLIUM.   PARIS, LOUVRE

THE PEREGRINE MUSE

STUDIES IN COMPARATIVE
RENAISSANCE LITERATURE

BY

ROBERT J. CLEMENTS

CHAPEL HILL

THE UNIVERSITY OF NORTH CAROLINA PRESS

To my friends and colleagues
GERMAINE BRÉE
OSCAR CARGILL
JOTHAM JOHNSON
ERNST ROSE
authors of the renaissance
in comparative literature
at New York University

FOREWORD

THE PEREGRINE muse of Italian Renaissance letters darted about Western Europe like a wanton St. Elmo's Fire. Some there were, like Guillaume Budé, who fretted over her ubiquities, even grumbling that she should be extradited. The wiser and more appreciative, like Shakespeare and Ronsard and Cervantes, happily accepted the favors of this Urania from time to time, without renouncing their own national troths. Most of the following essays illustrate the manner in which Italian letters influenced European writers from Ronsard up to Rilke. This is probably the one unity which can be claimed for the present volume.

Some of the material has been published in journals in America and Europe, and the first essay, which appeared in briefer form in Portugal, is the synopsis of a seminar given at the University of Madrid in 1953. Thanks for permission to reprint whole or partial texts are due the editors of the *Boletim do Museu Nacional da Arte Antiga* (Lisbon), *Romanic Review, Studies in Philology, Comparative Literature, Hispanic Review, Publications of the Modern Language Association, Italica, Modern Language Notes,* and the *Romanistisches Jahrbuch* (Hamburg).

Gratitude is expressed also to Professors U. T. Holmes and Sterling A. Stoudemire of the University of North Carolina for their interest in this project, to the administrators of the Clark Bequest of Harvard University, and to Dean Thomas C. Pollock of New York University and his fellow members of the Research Committee of the Graduate School of Arts and Sciences for their help in making the publication of this volume possible.

CONTENTS

THE
PEREGRINE MUSE

I

THE IDENTITY OF LITERARY AND ARTISTIC
THEORY IN THE RENAISSANCE

THE STUDY of Renaissance literary theory started on the very heels of interest in the Renaissance itself. Voigt, Burckhardt, Symonds, and Pater had scarcely finished their probings when the first histories of Renaissance literary criticism were issued by Pelletier, Langlois, Borinski, Grucker, and Vossler. Syntheses of Renaissance art theory were not to make an appearance until a half-century later, and the best investigations are by contemporaries still active at the present time—Venturi, Blunt, Lee, Panofsky—or in the discursive history of aesthetics by the regretted Menéndez y Pelayo, analyzing the Spanish tractatists on architecture and painting. A definitive survey of Renaissance art theory, comparable to the studies by Saintsbury and Spingarn for Renaissance literary theory, remains to be written. If such a compendium existed, expanding in depth and geographical breadth Anthony Blunt's pioneer little volume, *Artistic Theory in Italy, 1450-1600*, the task limned in this present essay would be much simplified. In any case, it becomes increasingly clear to anyone interested in both the literary and artistic speculations of the humanistic period that parallels in art theory and the theorizing on letters were unusually continuous and consistent and that a single set of aesthetic issues and problems was bequeathed to writers and artists alike, to be debated in much the same terms in academy and atelier. Only in recent times have facets of this identity been explored and its fascinating implications brought out. Notable contributions have been Erwin Panofsy's study of Platonism entitled *Idea*[1], Edgar Wind's much-debated interpretation of Bellini's *Feast of the Gods* as an echo of Ovid's Priapus,[2] and especially Rensselaer W. Lee's monograph which appeared in the *Art Bulletin* under the title "*Ut pictura poesis*: The Humanistic Theory of Painting."[3] Others, like Hatzfeld, have approached the identity of theory through keen observation of identity of practice. Thus he notes that in Poussin's *Les Philistins frappés de la peste*, only a man covering his nose will denote the ravages and

---

1. Erwin Panofsky, *Idea* (Leipzig, 1924).
2. Edgar Wind, *Bellini's Feast of the Gods* (Cambridge, Mass., 1948).
3. Rensselaer W. Lee, "*Ut Pictura Poesis*: The Humanistic Theory of Painting," *Art Bulletin*, XXII (1940) 197-269.

putrefaction of the plague, a concern for *bienséances* reminiscent of the offstage murder of Corneille's Camille or the offstage suicide of Racine's Hermione.[4] Indeed, the recent activity among scholars who have busied themselves analyzing the parallelism between literature and the arts has been surveyed by René Wellek, who reached the conclusion that "the problem should be approached anew,"[5] a conviction shared by Hatzfeld.[6]

Whether interested in identity of theory or of practice, these imaginative writers have left for a more final treatment the complete and sustained juxtaposition of literary and artistic speculation in the Renaissance. Such a study, following the lines set out in this essay, would measure not only the broad similarity of the general issues of humanistic or neoclassical doctrine reappearing in a Philip Sidney or a Giovan Paolo Lomazzo, for example, but would also proceed to the identity of imagery, metaphor, expression, and critical vocabulary.

It is paradoxical that no one has undertaken this exhaustive investigation, since the Renaissance was the very time that intellectuals were so happily misconstruing Horace's lines about *ut pictura poesis* and viewing art and poetry as equal creations of a single creative impulse. At this time everyone was busy improvising on the aphorism attributed by Plutarch to Simonides defining painting as mute poetry and poems as spoken pictures. Lomazzo, for example, translated the phrases as "poesia mutola" and "pittura loquace." An amusing improvisation is found in Lope's *Rimas del Licenciado Burguillos*, for example,

> Marino, gran pintor de los oídos,
> y Rubens, gran poeta de los ojos.[7]

This singleness of impulse, claimed Lomazzo, resulted in a "general conformity" not only of art and poetry, but also in an affinity between artists and poets. "For we see that Leonardo has expressed the movements and decorousness of Homer; Polidoro the grandeur and furor of Vergil; Buonarroti the deep obscurity of Dante; Raffaello the pure majesty of Petrarch; Andrea Mantegna the keen prudence of Sannazaro; Titian the variety of

---

4. Helmut Hatzfeld, "Literary Criticism through Art and Art Criticism through Literature," *Journal of Aesthetics and Art Criticism*, September, 1947, p. 12.

5. René Wellek, "The Parallel between Literature and the Arts," *The English Institute Annual* (New York, 1942), pp. 29-63.

6. Helmut Hatzfeld, *op. cit.*, p. 1.

7. Lope de Vega, *Rimas del Licenciado Burguillos* (Madrid, 1634), p. 56v.

Ariosto; and Gaudenzio the devotion which is found expressed in the books of the saints."[8] As we shall see below, Du Bellay will compare ,Michelangelo to a poet, as well—to his friend Pierre de Ronsard. It was said even in Michelangelo's time that his *Giudizio universale* had as its literary source the *Dies Irae*. It was an age when poets self-consciously imitated or rivaled works of art. Giovambattista Zappi "translated" Michelangelo's *Mosè* into a sonnet. Sadoletus strove to imitate the classic craftsmanship of the newly unearthed *Laokoon* in "elegant verse." Even though, as Lessing was to point out, the marble group itself was an imitation of a Vergilian passage. Venegas de Saavedra wrote a poem on Pacheco's portrait of Luciano de Negrón, while Soto de Rojas built a poem on Basano's *Crucifixion* and on Dürer's *Flight into Egypt*. We shall later presume that Ronsard or one of his contemporaries was so impressed by Michelangelo's bronze *David* as to translate a poem at its base.

It was an age when many writers and artists longed for the double kudos of the two professions. One thinks of the sonnet Lope directed to Jáuregui:

> Si en colores *Judit*, si en verso *Aminta*
> Duplicado laurel presumen darte,
> No es tu pluma, don Juan: escribe el arte;
> No es tu pincel; Naturaleza pinta.[9]

Legend had long since made Giotto a poet and Dante a painter. Lomazzo claimed that painters are driven by natural impulse to sing of their subjects in verse. He cites as example Bramante's enigma of the dice ("Usciron fuor dalle lor tombe oscure") and reproduces a sonnet by Leonardo.[10] He further lists as other poet-painters the "gymnosophists" Buonarroti, Ferrari, Luini, and the "Bernesque" Bronzino (who was, indeed, received among the humanists and writers of the Academy della Crusca).

Many formative influences of the time operated equally on poets and painters. Petrarchism and especially neo-Platonism affected poetic imagery just as they did the iconography of the artist. Abundantly shared themes were the androgyne, the ladder

8. Giovan Paolo Lomazzo, *Trattato dell'arte della pittura, scultura ed architettura* (Rome, 1844) II, 69.

9. Similarly, in his *Panegírico por la Poesía*, Fernando Vera y Mendoza praised the "láminas y versos" which made of Jáuregui "el honor de Sevilla" (Madrid, 1942), p. 71.

10. Lomazzo, *op. cit.*, II, 67-68.

of love, the Eros and Anteros, and the Platonic cosmography. When Francesco Berni writes of Michelangelo, "I've seen some of his compositions; I am ignorant and yet I should say that I've read all of them in the middle of Plato,"[11] he unconsciously fuses seeing and reading and syncretizes Buonarroti's literary and artistic creations as a single effort. Perhaps the most familiar Renaissance text where the poet unconsciously believed himself a sculptor is the strophe where Ariosto described Angelica as a nude model (as Ovid had depicted Andromeda) whom Lodovico had "feigned of alabaster or some other illustrious marble."[12]

Before enumerating the many issues of aesthetics upon which there was identity of opinion among the theorists on art and on letters, we should point out the homogeneity of even the treatises in which they circularized their ideas. The *ars pictoria* and the *are poetica* of the humanists were generally identical in structure. Divided into three or four "books" (i. e., chapters), the treatise started out with a speculative history of art or poetry, replete with erudite reminiscences. The first painter was the perspiring Christ, who painted his own portrait on Veronica's veil. The first poet was Orpheus, who tamed beasts, along with Amphion and Homer and Pindar, all practically contemporaries and all writing in Greek. (Pontus de Tyard was shocked that Orpheus knew only Greek.) The first book of the treatise or dialogue dealt also with such matters as whether painters and poets are born or made, and similar theorizing. Then the second book moved gradually toward practical instruction: the different types of painting (tempera, oil, fresco) and sculpture (bronze, marble, glyptics, clay) are listed, just as the several types of poetry were enumerated (ode, elegy, sonnet, epigram, *etc.*). Finally, because the theorists were so often practicing painters and poets, the final "book" gave useful instruction on details of technique and praxis (how to mix paints or how to count syllables). Whether the *ars poetica* actually preceded the *ars pictoria*, as is most probable, there is no doubt that both derived their ideas if not their structure from the same classical sources, primarily the poetics of Aristotle, Longinus, and Horace. Rensselaer Lee writes, "They did not hesitate to appropriate as the foundation of their own theory many basic concepts of the two ancient treatises (Aristotle

11. Quoted in Carl Frey, *Die Dichtungen des Michelagniolo* (Berlin, 1897), p. 263.

12. Indeed, Lessing's criticism of Ariosto in the *Laokoon* (decrying his depiction of Alcina) censures Lodovico even more as a painter than as a poet.

and Horace), making them apply in a more or less Procrustean manner to the art of painting for which they were never intended."[13] These *artes*, so alike in spirit and content, show the extent to which Condivi, Lomazzo, Dolce, and their confreres were undergoing the same influences as Vida, Du Bellay, Robortelli, and the literary theorists. Reading Paolo Pino's dialogue on painting and Boileau's tardy *Art poétique*, one is struck by the fact that two works conceived for entirely different audiences can both be *réchauffés* of Horace. In the High Renaissance Plato comes and joins the company of Aristotle and Horace as a unifier, bringing disparate types of influence to literary and artistic theory as he had to literature and art themselves. First of all, he brought along the theory of idealism by which so many recent students of Renaissance art and literature are now interpreting the major works of a Botticelli or a Maurice Scève. This aspect of Platonism so impregnated the poetic and pictorial arts that art theorists Lomazzo, Bellori, and Armenini called their critical expositions "Ideas" and the later poetics are somewhat lesser vehicles of Platonism.

The affinity of thinking in the *artes poeticae* and *pictoriae* was encouraged, then, by Horace's theory of *ut pictura poesis*, by Simonides's chiasmic comparison, by common source books, by the ideal of learned versatility in the Renaissance which was responsible for many painter-poets, and by habits of analogy which led Lomazzo, for example, to claim that painting and verse were "quasi nate ad un parto." As for the widespread influence of the *ut pictura poesis* phrase, we shall show below how frequently it recurred in just one branch of Renaissance literature, emblem literature, without attempting to chart the spread of the cliché among the writers on art or through the treatises of such theorists as Minturno, Tasso, and Castelvetro.

The basic issue upon which the theorists agreed was the mimetic nature of art and literature. Lomazzo, for example, finds them both "studiose imitatrici della natura delle cose, e degli accidenti loro, in quanto è lor dato."[14] Not only did the humanists follow Plato's line that art and letters were imitations of imitations, but they agreed in accepting the two principal values of the word imitation. Said Vasari, "L'arte nostra è tutta imitazione, della natura principalmente, e poi, perchè da sè non può salir tanto alto, delle cose che da quelli che miglior maestri di sè giudica son

13. Rensselaer W. Lee, *op. cit.*, p. 201.
14. Lomazzo, *op. cit.*, II, 468.

condotte."[15] The earliest reference to Aristotelian mimesis was in the third book of Trissino's poetics in 1529, although this concept was not widely understood inside or outside Italy until mid-century. The second type of imitation, plagiarism, was also commonly endorsed by the literary theorists, Vida encouraging poets to steal liberally from other writers. Just as one reads in his poetics

> Ergo agite o mecum securi accingite furtis
> Una omnes, pueri, passimque avertite praedam,[16]

so may one read in Dolce's dialogue on painting that "one should imitate the beautiful marble or bronze figures of the antique masters . . . for things of antiquity contain all the perfection of art and can be exemplars of all that is beautiful."[17] Just as it was agreed by the theorists that a young sculptor would imitate the treatment of surfaces of the Belvedere Torso or that a painter should learn his profession by copying the Masaccio frescoes in the Cappella Brancacci of Santa Maria del Carmine in Florence, so was it understood that a fledgling poet would plagiarise any great archetype from Pindar to Petrarch.

Once the poet or painter borrowed elements from his masters or models, he endeavored to distill or absorb them in a process which Faguet has called innutrition. Plato's *Ion* supplied the theorists with the most apt image to describe the process, for Plato reminded them that lyric poets "gather their strains from honeyed fountains out of the gardens and dells of the Muses; thither, like bees, they wend their way."[18] Thus a whole generation of Renaissance literary theorists adopted the metaphor of the bee, as did Ronsard in his *Hylas*, to justify and illustrate the culling process.[19] We are not surprised therefore to find the honey-bee image reappearing as applied to the fine arts. Condivi describes Michelangelo as "choosing the beautiful from nature, as the bees gather honey from flowers, making use of it later in their works."[20]

Associated with the issue of plagiarism is the Quarrel of the Ancients and Moderns, no less animated among the art theorists than among the literati. As we know from their use of *rinascita*

15. Giorgio Vasari, *Le Vite* (Florence, 1878-82), I, 222.
16. Vida, *De arte poetica*, iii, 243-44.
17. Lodovico Dolce, *Dialogo della Pittura* (Florence, 1735), p. 190.
18. Plato, *Ion*, Jowett translation (New York, 1936) V, i, 533d.
19. Pierre de Ronsard, *Œuvres* (Paris, 1914-19) V, 132.
20. Ascanio Condivi, *Vita di Michelangelo* (Pisa, 1823), p. 80.

and kindred words, the theorists on art and even on literature were well aware that they lived in a period of rebirth, reflowering, renewal. Indeed, Vasari's use of *rinascita* and Lomazzo's and Armenini's use of equivalent coinages viewed the new Golden Age strictly in terms of the arts of design, to delimit the age of Raphael and Michelangelo. It was generally agreed that one could approach the ancients and even, in rare cases, equal them. Thus Ronsard could justly be called the new Pindar (although in a moment of rare humility he demanded that the muse of his *Franciade* genuflect to Homer's muse) and Raphael be hailed as the new Apelles. But because of the curious contemporary psychology, both the *ars poetica* and *pictoria* reached the independent conclusion that, in spite of contemporary hyperbole and flattery, one could not surpass Homer or Zeuxis. The reason can be expressed syllogistically,

Thesis: Ancient writers or artists were so close to nature and divinity as to become natural or divine to a greater degree than is possible in modern times.
Antithesis: A modern cannot surpass nature or divinity.
Synthesis: A modern cannot surpass ancient poets or artists.

Vasari explains it in this way: "Quei primi uomini, i quali quanto manco erano lontani dal suo principio e divina generazione, tanto erano più perfetti e di migliore ingegno, essi per loro avendo per guida la natura."[21] Bellori expresses the same idea in Platonic language, urging the careful study of ancient statuary, since antique artists "had used the marvelous Idea."[22] It was the same with the archaic poets. Du Bellay relates how Hesiod took one draught from the spring of Hippocrene and was changed from herdsman into perfect poet. Rivers were no longer able to do this in the sixteenth century. The closeness to nature of the *Urdichter* is indeed the initial theme of Ronsard's splendid *Ode à Michel de l'Hospital:*

> Divins, d'autant que la nature
> Sans art librement exprimoient:
> Sans art leur naive escriture
> Par la fureur ils animoyent.[23]

The fictive nature of the creative process was viewed in the same terms by the artistic and literary theorists. Dante and Boccaccio had claimed that *poiéo* in Greek had been supplanted in

21. Giorgio Vasari, *Le Vite, ed. cit.,* I, 222.
22. Giovan Battista Bellori, *Le Vite dei pittori, scultori, ed archittetori,* quoted in E. Panosky, *Idea* (Leipzig, 1924), p. 137.
23. Pierre de Ronsard, *ed. cit.,* II, 139.

Latin by *fingo*. By the time of Vida *fingere* had become the standard verb to describe the poetic process, but now bore connotations
of feigning or veiling or cloaking (Stephan Hawes). Ronsard
states that he has learned the art of poetry from Jean Dorat,
acknowledging that the elder humanist "m'apprist la poésie, et
me monstra comment / on doit feindre et cacher les fables propre-
ment."[24] The notion that poetry must veil truth infiltrated the
thinking on art, of course. Du Bellay, for example, wrote that
Ronsard and Michelangelo were kindred spirits and "with an
unlimited art, hide truth under a thousand fictions,"[25] adding
that poets who write things as they are will be inferior to those
who feign. Leon Battista Alberti, in his *Della Pittura*, asserted
that one must "fingiere quello che si vede."[26] Lomazzo's *Idea
del tempio della Pittura* concedes to painters a "license to feign
and invent"[27] and justifies their creating a veil *(velame)* in
feigning. Again in his *Trattato dell'arte* the same critic held that
Michelangelo's idealizing manner constituted use of the "veil of
art" *(velo dell'arte)*, and Dolce saw Michelangelo imitating
the philosophers who veiled truths. The Venetian Paolo Pino
has the spokesman Fabio in his *Dialogo di Pittura* state that
poetry and painting are alike in "making appear what is not."
Their mutual properties and aims of hiding, obscuring, cloaking,
and deceiving gave rise to proverbs about their mendacity. The
most common was probably *licet poetis mentire*, and if an equally
endemic proverb concerning lying artists does not come to mind,
we can at least locate the idea in one of those sententious and pithy
collections of Renaissance folk wisdom: the emblem books. In a
curious volume issued at Augsburg in 1536, *Das Buch Schimpff
unnd Ernst*, appeared this nugget of popular wisdom:

Es ist ein sprichwort: Poetis & pictoribus est eadem potestas. Die maler und
Poeten haben gleychen gewalt. Die maler achten keiner warheyt inn dem malen
allein dass es wol stand. Die poeten achten auch keiner wahrheyt allein das man
sehe das sie auch Latein kundten reden.[28]

If we return to Du Bellay's statement that Ronsard and Michelangelo, unlike Pierre Paschal and Clouet, "hide truth under
a thousand fictions," Michelangelo's *Saettatori* would seem to be
a splendid example, even though Ronsard's feigning never
equalled that of, let us say, the unauthenticated author Colonna

24. *Ibid.*, IV, 313.
25. Joachim du Bellay, *Œuvres poétiques* (Paris, 1931) VI, 164-65.
26. Leon Battista Alberti, *Della Pittura* (Florence, 1950), p. 55.
27. Lomazzo, *Idea del tempio della Pittura* (Milan, 1590), p. 36.
28. *Das Buch Schimpff unnd Ernst* (Augsburg, 1536). n. p.

of the *Hypnerotomachia Poliphili*. The *Archers* and the *Dream of Poliphilus* fall into the category of allegory, that mediaeval practice which persisted into the Renaissance. It was natural that allegory should bring the poet and artist together, since allegory is born of a habit of seeing graphically and vividly. No treatise on painting claimed for art the four levels of meaning which Dante alleged for poetry. But both poets and painters were conscious of the obligation to express two meanings: literal and allegorical on the part of the poets, and photographic (facsimile) and iconological on the part of painters and sculptors. The whole panoply of symbols of protero-Christian art was still present in the churches and rituals. If muse or memory failed a poet or painter, he had recourse to works like the *Iconology* of Ripa, the *Hieroglyphics* of Horapollo, the *Emblems* of Alciati, or even the mythological *Imagines* of Cartarus in his search for the appropriate symbols with which to embellish his book or his canvas. Neoclassicism, declaring that the characters of tragedy or sculpture should not be individuals, but rather abstract typoi, universals, made symbols of them. As symbols they confounded literal minds: the Virgin of the Vatican *Pietà* of Michelangelo resembles the younger sister of the dead Christ lying in her arms, whereas Phaedra, symbol of the "distracted mother," as our British cousins subtitled their translation of the Racinian play, was also too young to serve as model of a mother. Since Hellenic literature afforded examples of allegorical writings, contrasted with little allegory in their art, some in the Renaissance believed that artistic allegory was the consequence of literary allegory. Lodovico Dolce attests this in the following exchange from his *Dialogo della Pittura:*

Giovan Francesco Fabrini: For I have heard it said that in the order of his stupendous *Last Judgment* are contained several deep allegorical meanings understood by few.

Pietro Aretino: In this he deserves great praise, since it appears that in this he imitated those great philosophers who hid under the veil of poesy the greatest mysteries of philosophy.[29]

Invention was another issue treated frequently in the treatises on art and on poetry. Paolo Pino's *Dialogo di Pittura* makes a trinity of painting, poetry, and invention. "La Pittura è propria Poesia, cioè Invenzione."[30] One mutually proposed notion was that invention was merely the discovery of forms inherent in

29. Lodovico Dolce, *Dialogo della Pittura* (Florence, 1735), pp. 242, 246.
30. Paolo Pino, *Dialogo di Pittura* (Venice, 1946), pp. 105-7.

the materials of nature, or of *concetti* originally planned and created by God. The idea originated with Michelangelo and the neo-Platonists (Michelangelo even declaring that predetermined Ideas exist in the writer's ink), but was voiced also by Galileo, Desportes, and others. It was tied in with the principle of *trobar clus*, or the "finding" of the troubadours. However, by this belief the artist and writer relinquish practically all of their *liber arbitrium* as inventive intellects to either a Platonic or a Christian God. It remained more popular to concede that gods gave artists genius and the latter did their own inventing. The theorists often cited Horace's famous justification of the poet's and artist's inventive freedom and poetic license: "Pictoribus atque poetis / Quidlibet audendi semper fuit aequa potestas." Indeed, the artist-poet Michelangelo quotes the verses from memory to Diego Zapata, applauds them, and then explains in which ways this license may make its pact with versimilitude.[31]

Naturally, there are cautions about invention in both the *ars poetica* and the *ars pictoria*. The constant reminder to the playwrights that kings must talk in a princely way is paralleled in counsel to painters that kings must be noble in appearance and raiment. Such parallels are legion. Much more vivid than the counsels in the treatises are the attacks on the poets and painters of the Renaissance by their contemporaries who feel they have abused their poetic license. The attacks on religious grounds make most interesting reading: Gilio da Fabriano scoring Michelangelo for painting wind-blown standards on the Day of Judgment (when winds will cease); the papal censor reprimanding writers like Montaigne for using the word fortune (rather than providence); the Inquisitional star-chamber indictment of Veronese for introducing dogs, dwarfs, and soldiers into his *Feast in the House of Levi*. Sometimes the indictments are on other grounds than religious. Lope de Vega was so irritated by the exclusion of Spanish crusaders in Tasso's epic that he complained and then set out to rewrite the epic himself.

The issue of the dignity of art and literature comes up often in the two types of treatise we are discussing. This is more understandable when we realize that in both fields the theorists were most often practitioners. The theorist-practitioners in Italy are well-known—Ghiberti, Da Vinci, Vasari, Lomazzo, Tasso, Vida, and others. Spain, too, affords conspicuous examples. Lope wrote plays, poetry, and a treatise on comedies; Jáuregui painted and

31. Francisco de Hollanda, *Dialogos em Roma* (Porto, 1918), pp. 231-32.

theorized; Juan de Arpha was a gold- and metalsmith and theorist on the art of drawing. This coincidence accounted for the emphatic insistence that poets and artists had an important social function. They confer immortality upon men of virtue. Sometimes poets and artists joined forces in this endeavor as they did in preparing several Renaissance editions of *Icones virorum illustrium.* Or they could perform this function separately. Ronsard informally assures a king of France that without Pindaric odes that monarch's renown would be engulfed by death in the black Stygian mud, while Leon Battista Alberti reminds his readers that "the faces of the dead live, in a sense, a lengthy life by means of painting."[32] And did not Lomazzo specify that poets and painters alike "have illustrious deeds as their objects, and praises of heroes to represent"?[33] The persistence of the Horatian line, "exegi monumentum aere perennius," was the goading reminder that writings outlast monuments, as was the proverb "scripta manent," but the theorists on both art and letters recognized the power of the pen and the brush as instrumental in bringing dignity to the two professions.

The dignity of both painters and poets fluctuated with the Maecenate system, which could threaten their new and hard-won status or even reduce them to the role of tradesmen or craftsmen rather than members of a profession. It was humiliating to have to compose an epithalamium to a distant or unknown relative of one's patron or to compose love sonnets or *bacia* for a Henri III, describing caresses and kisses that another was receiving, like Cyrano writing for Christian. Just as perilous to one's dignity was the requirement of having to waste one's talents on portraits, which were the Pindaric odes of painting. Or to have to spend one's time making a snowman, as Michelangelo was required to do for young Piero de' Medici. It was not merely one's personal *amour propre* which was at stake in these cases, but rather the dignity of an entire profession.

Thus, aware that poets and painters could degrade themselves and their vocations for money, the critics and theorists busily reminded them (and often themselves as practitioners) that they must show disdain for wealth. Vida's poetics carried the reminder, "Hic laeti haud magnis opibus, non divite cultu vitam agitant vates, . . ."[34] Jean-Antoine de Baïf said of the true poet,

32. Alberti, *Della Pittura* (Milan, 1804), p. 37.
33. Lomazzo, *Trattato, ed. cit.,* II, 67.
34. Vida, *De arte poetica,* i, 492-93.

"Ni aux richesses il ne baille."[35] And Cervantes advised the poet in his *Viaje del Parnaso*, "No procura a llegar a rico, como a honroso estado."[36] The art theorists echo this disdain for riches claiming to prefer with Alberti "praise, grace, and benevolence." The artists themselves disclaim that they are artists "who keep a shop." In Paolo Pino's dialogue the speakers exclude such artists from their discussion: "Di quegli che attendono a porre i bei colori in opera per trarre i quattrini, io non intendo parlarne."[37] Da Vinci refuses to hire as assistant an artist who keeps a public shop, while Michelangelo cries, "Io non fu' mai pittore nè scultore come chi ne fa bottega."[38]

For a variety of reasons, including the new discovery of ancient poetry, the poet could be sure of social prestige sooner than the artist. "But the painters and sculptors did not content themselves with a general claim to learning," writes Anthony Blunt,[39] "they explicitly demanded equality with poets. Poetry and rhetoric were accepted as liberal arts, and the painters and sculptors evidently felt that, if they could show that their arts were as noble as that of the poets, they would have proved their claim to be liberal artists also. The first difficulty which they had to overcome was that painting and sculpture seemed to be more manual than literature. Equicola, for instance, says: 'Therefore, however worthy of praise painting, modeling, and sculpture may be, nevertheless they must be considered far inferior to poetry in dignity and authority. Painting is a work and a labour more of the body than of the mind and is, more often than not, exercised by the ignorant.' Leonardo, however, has a reply ready for this kind of argument; and in defence of painting he says, 'If you call it mechanical because it is, in the first place, manual, and it is the hand which produces what is to be found in the imagination, you writers also set down manually with the pen what is devised in your mind.'

"Having dealt with this attack," Blunt continues, "Leonardo goes on to claim that the painter can achieve no less than the poet.

35. Jean-Antoine de Baïf, *Œuvres en rime* (Paris, 1881-90) II, 392.

36. And it was Cervantes who declared that the worldly possessions of a poet could be carried on the back of a pack-mule.

37. Paolo Pino, *Dialogo di Pittura* (Venice, 1946), also says that the artist who deigns to "far mercato" debases his art (p. 154).

38. Leonardo da Vinci, *Notebooks* (New York, 1939), p. 1132; Milanesi edition of Michelangelo's letters (Florence, 1875), p. 225.

39. Anthony Blunt, *Artistic Theory in Italy, 1450-1600* (Oxford, 1956), pp. 51-52.

Painting can represent an action as completely, more completely even, than poetry; and, in particular, painting can attain the same moral ends on which poetry prides itself." We shall come back in turn to the questions of learning and of morality. For the moment we have to admit that nothing could irritate great artists so much as to be considered manual workers. In 1542 Michelangelo wrote to an unknown prelate at the court of Paul III, "Io rispondo che si dipinge col ciervello et non con le mani."[40] Nor did that well-intended but ingenuous strophe please or flatter him which Fausto Sabeo sent to him, with its verse, "Fingimus, ingenio namque ego, tuque manu."[41] It would not be difficult to set up an inventory of these protests by the Renaissance artists whose art was, in the words of Leonardo, "una cosa mentale."

Just as Sidney and others insisted that poetry is one of the liberal arts, equal to its two principal detractors, philosophy and history, so did Ghiberti and succeeding theorists claim that painting is a lofty art. Indeed, Pino calls it a "species of natural philosophy," the exact phrase applied to it by Da Vinci. Then, although poets and artists might dispute among themselves which was the greater profession (Ronsard cannot refrain from complaining that architects won a better living than poets) both groups demanded and obtained recognition as members of a noble liberal profession.

The artists' new pretensions to learning, mentioned above by Blunt, showed that they had been successfully indoctrinated by the writers of treatises on the fine arts. Just as the treatises on poetry hailed the ideal of the *doctus poeta* who would know "toutes sciences" (Ronsard) or "every form of human learning" (Minturno), so did the *artes pictoriae* spell out exactly which branches of knowledge were essential to the artist. A sampling of three of the Italian chapbooks follows:[42]

Leon Battista Alberti, *Della Pittura*: geometry, rhetoric, poetry, history, "all the liberal arts."

Lorenzo Ghiberti, *I Commentarii*: Grammar, geometry, philosophy, medicine, astrology, perspective, history, anatomy, theory of design, arithmetic.

Giovan Paolo Lomazzo, *Idea del tempio della Pittura*: theology, mathematics, astrology, geometry, arithmetic, architecture, music, poetry, anatomy, philosophy, and others.

40. Gaetano Milanesi, *Le Lettere di Michelangelo* (Florence, 1875), p. 489.
41. In James Hutton, *The Greek Anthology in Italy* (Ithaca, 1935), p. 213.
42. Alberti, *Della Pittura*, Book III; Ghiberti, *ed. cit.*, p. 4; Lomazzo, *Idea*, *ed. cit.*, pp. 33-34.

We have seen how poetic and artistic license was frequently curtailed by religious censure or disapproval. The Reformational and counter-Reformational attacks on literature and the fine arts gave strength to the old Platonic suspicions of the creative arts. The Tridentine Council, legislating against unorthodoxy and indecency, could question the very reason-for-existence of a poem or a picture. Just as fear of censure by Annibal Caro or other clerical authorities drove Tasso to rewrite the *Gerusalemme lib-erata* as *conquistata* and to metamorphose his knights and mistresses into priests and nuns, so did five popes decide to "rewrite" Michelangelo's *Giudizio universale*. And poor, devoted Daniele da Volterra was ordered, to the snickering of the people of Rome, to put loin bibs on the nudes. Just as religious mobs under Savonarola threw works of painting on the Dominican friar's Pyre of Vanities, so did religious zealots in Lyon sack the home of Castelvetro and destroy his *Commentary on Plato, Critique on the Comedies of Terence and Plautus*, the translation of the *New Testament*, and *Commentary on the Divina Commedia*. The *libre examen* of Scripture, often denied the literary people of the Renaissance, was also forbidden the painters. The Spanish Inquisition condemned Torrigiano to death for painting against doctrine and hounded poor Francisco Sánchez de las Brozas for "faulty" rendering of the Last Supper ("era costumbre que los privados se llegasen a la cabeça del Señor del conuite, . . ."). And when Veronese was brought to trial because his version of the *Feast in the House of Simon* was at variance with the Bible (see above), the Tribunal of the Inquisition was unmoved by Veronese's apology, based on the *ut pictura poesis:* "We painters take the same licenses that the poets and jesters take." The dominion of the Council of Trent over art and letters is discussed in detail in Charles Dejob's venerable volume, *De l'Influence du Concile de Trente sur la littérature et les beaux-arts chez les peuples catholiques.*

Religious themes were being urged upon artists by the Maecenate system, for the Church in the Renaissance was the greatest employer of artists. *Pictura laicorum Scriptura.* Once Michelangelo became attached to Julius II, he never again did a major lay subject with the single exception of the *Brutus.* Yet the writers were also being counseled on all sides to choose religious topics. Jean Mauguin advised,

Chantez d'accord, du Puissant Dieu des Dieux
La grand' doulceur de sa misericorde.[43]

He used much the same terms Du Bartas used, making the same plea in his *Uranie*. Henry Peacham urged the Anglican poets to do the same:

Bid now, my Muse, thy lighter task adieu,
As shaken blossome of a better fruite,
And with Urania thy Creator view,
To sing of Him, or evermore be mute. . . .[44]

Even Ronsard, the French reincarnation of Pindar and Anacreon, reminded his colleagues that poetry is a handmaid to theology, that poets should glorify God to "faire connaître aux peuples ignorans les excellences de sa majesté."[45] In Spain Juan Luis Vives recommended religious themes in his poetics years before the *Christiada* by the Sevillian Hojeda (1611), and the repertory of Spanish pinacotecas abounds in the saints and angels that Vives prescribed for poetry, saints whose sufferings and ecstasies make up the force of Spanish baroque. Don Luis did not dream that four years after his death a Frenchman would be born to write a baroque epic *(Les Tragiques)* depicting the sufferings and ecstasies of Protestant martyrs, sufferings which never did, however, find their painter. In general, it was the Catholic rather than the schismatic theorists who insisted upon religious themes in the old Scholastic tradition, and the Anglican Richard Crashaw had to conclude that "Saint Teresa is well worth a mass."

Theorists on both letters and arts agreed that practitioners must be men of morality and virtue. Minturno has written that since the poet is a teacher of virtue, he must be a virtuous man; if he is not a good man, he will not write good poetry. This idea, by the way, came out of an oft-quoted passage in Strabo's geography. Vasari, Lomazzo, and Michelangelo all echoed that art comes more easily and fittingly to chaste men, and Savonarola preached that "debauched men are the enemies of the fine arts."[46] In his dialogue on painting, Paolo Pino exclaims simply, "Let the painter be a good Christian!"[47] Being good Christians, the poet and the artist often found that the task of instilling virtue

43. Jean Mauguin, *Les Figures de l'Apocalypse* (Paris, 1547) final unnumbered page.
44. Henry Peacham, *Minerva Britanna* (London, 1612), p. 177.
45. Pierre de Ronsard, *ed. cit.*, VII, 44.
46. Girolamo Savonarola, *Predica XVI sul Salmo: "Quam bonus."*
47. Paolo Pino, *Dialogo di Pittura, ed. cit.*, pp. 32, 35.

through their works was made more difficult by the need of their aristocratic patrons for titillation, those patrons of the Renaissance so scathingly arraigned by Tolstóy in *What is Art?*

The positivistic forces of history induced both poets and artists to make a cult of nobility. The ideal of the lofty tone which went back to Longinus and even Aristotle influenced artists as well as authors. This was one of the rare cases where a precept of rhetoric made itself an ideal of art. The ideal of sublimity supposed a lofty style and form. Furthermore, the doctrine of sublimity supposed that arts and letters dealt with figures of rank, with "praestantiores." Alberti, Vasari, and Armenini all remembered that in antiquity persons of low station had not been permitted to learn art.[48] This requirement of the *altiloque*, which some read into Aristotle, was applied especially to the epic poem and tragedy, whose position among the literary genres was comparable to that of painting and sculpture among the arts of design, as the fine arts were then called. The nobles of Thebes and Rome stepped onto the theatrical boards as well as the canvases. Jodelle dedicated a tragedy to Cleopatra, just as Shakespeare did later, and Michelangelo chose this queen for one of his "teste divine." The system of the Maecenate favored noble themes as well (the best ode of Ronsard was written to the Chancellor of France) and sent the artists off to do portraits of the highborn, an expedient and a concession which irritated the greatest masters. In Iberia, more aware of chivalry and more conscious of social classes, the painting of portraits retained its nobility of subject even after losing its nobleness of style. This, at least, one gathers from the *desornamentado* style, especially in the painting of Sánchez Coello, who painted the Princess Eboli with a patch of black cloth covering her blind eye. Thus the sublimity of the high Renaissance makes a compromise with the secular realism of the Spains. The *parti pris* of the poet and artist favoring the noble resulted from a lack of social consciousness. If philosophy, literature, science, and art made tremendous strides during the Renaissance, social progress and a sense of social justice and egalitarian spirit had not advanced much since the period of feudal society. Machiavelli was preferred to Etienne de la Boétie or to Jean Bodin, antagonists of dictators. After we have accepted the *Brutus* of Michelangelo as concrete approval of tyrannicide, we find Buonarroti in the dialogues of Donato Giannotti explaining that the Roman senator should never have killed Julius Caesar after all.

48. Vasari, *Le Vite, ed. cit.,* I, 219.

Despite the claim of Diego Rivera, the Renaissance never produced a Goya or a Daumier, just as it never produced a Zola or a Galdós. Humanism had not yet arrived at humanitarianism, which was to inform literature only two centuries later.

An American scholar, Vernon Hall, was the first to posit that Renaissance literary theory and criticism were upperclass and dictated chiefly by socio-political motives. In *Renaissance Literary Criticism: A Study of its Social Content* he studies in turn the literary theories of Italy, France, and England, showing in the case of each how social and political convictions and prejudices affected the contemporary views on language, genres, decorum, the role of the poet and the function of poetry. (Sample reasonings: decorum reproduces in poetry the class distinctions of society; tragedy is the highest genre because it treats of aristocratic characters.) To uphold his thesis the author assembles a weighty collection of quotations in Italian, French, English, and Latin. A most interesting challenge is thus made to the student of aesthetics to compose a similar work on the parallel thesis that "the thinking of the art critics, based upon an acceptance of the social hierarchy then existing, was dominated by the aristocratic viewpoint."

Another favorite theme of the tractatists on art and literature was genres. The famous Paragon which interested Varchi and Leonardo so much has its parallel in literary discussions. The quarrel over the primacy of tragedy or epic was as old as Aristotle, but by now the primacy of painting or sculpture was mooted even more. Michelangelo's compromise position, opposing Leonardo's, was that painting became superior to the extent that it resembled sculpture. A parallel compromise was made by such theorists as Tasso, who held that the best elements of tragedy could also be found in the epic poem. Were they aware of the identity of the cathedral and the epic?[49] We have not found a Renaissance precursor of Menéndez y Pelayo, saying "La Poesía, la Escultura, y la Pintura iban destronando a toda prisa á aquel arte sintética y de grandes masas que había levantado los gigantescos poemas de piedra de la Edad Media. Rota la unidad espiritual que les había inspirado, el genio individual se sobreponía al colectivo, y tanto la epopeya como la Arquitectura, artes una

49. It was Menéndez Pelayo who defined "cathedral" as "poema más espléndido de los siglos medios," *Historia de las ideas estéticas en España* (Santander, 1940) I, 480.

y otra anónimas por su esencia, cedían ante la invasión del genio
lírico y poético."

Like musicians improvising on themes, the theorists on art and
letters explore to the fullest the repertory of classical images
and figures which express the operation of the phenomena of
inspiration: Apollo, muses, demons (Lorca's *duende* is from an
old family) fury, Parnassus, Hippocrene, Permessus, and all
that Boeotian topography. The idea of creative fury, for example,
revived after the translations of the *Phaedrus*, was naturally applied to painters and sculptors, even though architects remained
invulnerable to these God-breathings. Lomazzo, who so frequently drew analogies between poets and painters, observed,
"Painters are in many parts similar to poets, especially since in
painting as in poetising there runs the Apollinic fury."[50] Perhaps the most interesting discussion of poetic fury is in Pontus
de Tyard's lengthy and little-read essay, "Premier solitaire, ou
Discours des Muses et de la fureur poétique," which defines
poetic fury Platonically: "l'unique escalier par lequel l'âme
peut trouver le chemin qui la conduise à la source de son souverain
bien & félicité dernière."[51] Ronsard's significant "La Lyre"
describes vividly the entire cycle of seizure by this fury. Cellini
claimed that Michelangelo created best under a *furia* or *furore*,
and another contemporary claimed that Buonarroti did the *Noli
me tangere* cartoon *in furia*.[52] Even astrology continued to explain
why some had genius and others did not. The Venetian Paolo Pino
declares, "We are guided to such perfection by means of a good
disposition of nature which reaches inside us by certain conjunctures of the planets more propitious at our conception or at our
birth."[53] Indeed, Condivi attributes the prodigious talent of Buonarroti to one of these benign conjunctures.[54] Two most important poems of the time—if we acknowledge the fact that only bien-
astré poets could be good poets—were Ronsard's "Hymne des astres" and his "Hymme des estoiles." Despite the scorn of some, including Rabelais, for astrology and its alleged powers, the literary
and artistic writers included it in their speculations on genius.
Even Boileau, that elegant plagiarist, immortalized this relationship in the initial pages of his *Art poétique*.

50. Lomazzo, *Trattato, ed. cit.,* II, 67.
51. Pontus de Tyard, *Discours philosophiques* (Paris, 1587), fol. 8r.
52. Benvenuto Cellini, *Due trattati* (Milan, 1811), p. 213.
53. Paolo Pino, *Dialogo di Pittura, ed. cit.,* p. 143.
54. Condivi, *Vita di Michelangelo* (Pisa, 1823), iv.

This panoply of images of inspiration rather assumed that poets and artists are the products of the direct intervention of nature, and minimize the necessity of training, instruction, exercise, praxis, effort, and sweat. Painters as well as poets consented to believe in the supremacy of innate genius, but remained aware that grinding and mixing colors, blocking out and cutting marbles, or counting syllables and adhering to a metric pattern had to be learned and practiced, making nature and art equal participants in the formation of genius. In the garden of Genius, as Cervantes wrote:

> Naturaleza y arte allí parece
> Andar en competencia, y está en duda
> Cuál vence de las dos, cuál más merece.[55]

That the literary theorists who dealt with this controversy reached a compromise position is apparent from their many allusions to "instructed muses" and to "learned demons" and from statements like the following in Louis le Caron's dialogue, "Ronsard, ou De la Poésie": "La Nature et l'Art sont les dons communs de Dieu, sans lesquels le poète ne doit espérer de rendre quelque œuvre louable et excellente."[56] And speaking for the arts of design, Leon Battista Alberti declared that "one must never set down to work without the escort of genius, and yet be taught and trained as well."[57]

We have dealt thus far with most of the major topics of Renaissance literary theory and aesthetics. Let us look for a moment and see how agreement was reached on two or three minor but more specific issues. Even on the matter of katharsis there was an equal acceptance. This purgation, served up by the scientist-doctor Aristotle as the very mechanism justifying the existence of creative literature, was a major element of Renaissance literary theory; one also finds echoes of it in the speculations on art. Pity, fear, and even that third element of cleansing, awe, were the aims of the artists as well, charged with their Christian mission. Even before the upsurge of Baroque, Crucifixions were the most common of the pitiful themes, and Leonardo da Vinci wrote sarcastically in his notebooks, "What! Christ crucified again!" Michelangelo, one of the few who did not

55. Miguel de Cervantes, *Viaje del Parnaso*, iii, 436-38.
56. Louis le Caron, "Ronsard, ou De la Poésie," quoted in Marcel Raymond, *L'Influence de Ronsard* (Paris, 1927) I, 316.
57. Alberti, *Della Pittura, ed. cit.*, p. 93.

paint or carve a Crucifixion, understood all too well the searing experience of katharsis, as Panofsky has noted. The artist wrote,

> Se 'l duol fa pur, com' alcun dice, bello,
> Privo piangendo d'un bel volto umano,
> L'esser infermo è sano,
> Fa vita e gratia la disgrazia mia.[58]

Not that the pathos of classical themes did not run a close second, as was well known to the tragic poets of the Camerata dei Bardi, for example. So tremendous was the impact of the *Laokoon* that it was copied not only by El Greco, the great purgator, but even by poets like Sadoletus, as already noted.

Another minor element of Renaissance thinking was the Horatian advice, "Sumite materiam vestris aequam viribus." It was found repeatedly in the poetic treatises after Vida and echoed in the treatises on art. It found poetic articulation by none other than Leonardo, in his sonnet:

> Chi non puo quel che vuol, quel che puo voglia;
> Che quel che non si puo, folle è volere.[59]

Or again it might be found in Alberti's counsel, "To try to keep doing more than you really can or more than is suitable is the sign of a talent rather obstinate than diligent."[60] Or, finally, Michelangelo's remark in the garden of the convent on San Silvestro: "And hereby one recognizes the wisdom of a great man, in the fear with which he does that thing which he understands the best; and conversely, the ignorance of others in the audacious temerity with which they encumber pictures with what they really cannot learn to do."[61]

Many parallels of thinking could be found on the matter of decorum. As we shall observe in a later chapter, López Pinciano's poetic treatise frowns upon such words as *jarro* appearing in plays. Gilio da Fabriano does not approve of a horse's croup appearing on canvas. Such squeamishness will lead to the sterile academism of neoclassical court painters like Vigée Lebrun on the one hand, and to the apology by Joseph Warton that the translation of Vergil must of necessity reproduce such coarse words as "plough," "sow," "wheat," and "dung."

Of course, the coincidence of practice in poetry and painting

58. Carl Frey, *Die Dichtungen des Michelagniolo, ed. cit.,* p. 223.
59. Lomazzo, *Trattato, ed. cit.,* II, 68.
60. Alberti, *Della Pittura, ed. cit.,* p. 97.
61. Francisco de Hollanda, *Dialogos em Roma, ed. cit.,* p. 240.

reached a very special intensity during the Baroque phase of the Renaissance. It is possible to take the passage on the assumption of the Protestant martyrs in D'Aubigné's *Tragiques* (III, 109-122) beginning "Là les bandes du ciel, humbles, agenouillées, Présentèrent à Dieu mil ames despouillées" and find it teeming with such common Baroque characteristics as energy, emphasis, violence, horror, martyrdom, theatricality, the *merveilleux chrétien*, concreteness, incarnation, refulgence, synaesthesia, ecstasy, contrast, disguise, and metamorphosis, just as one finds them in the Spanish paintings of martyrdom. Or to take the case of Richard Crashaw, as worded by Wylie Sypher, "Crashaw's 'Stabat Mater' is like a Murillo Purísima, where both worlds take part in the sensuous drama of baroque art, and his 'Prayer' is a gesture from Sassoferrato or Carlo Dolci."[62] Helmut Hatzfeld has demonstrated brilliantly in an article on the Baroque "problem" how baroque literature and art are dedicated, *inter alia*, to chiaroscuro, citing on the one hand the contrast of light and shade in Tasso, Gongora, Cervantes, and Racine, and on the other Rembrandt and Michelangelo.[63]

However, our interest is not in showing how poetry and painting elucidated or paralleled each other in the Renaissance. We are concerned with theory rather than practice, the coincidence of theory in the conventional vehicles of speculation: the *artes*, prefaces, pamphlets, or other written sources. So far as Baroque is concerned, no theorist during its *Blütezeit* was able to recognize and formulate its varied and yet consistent principles. There were a few individual statements of significance: Luis Vives' charge that poets and painters should treat of Christian martyrs, Gilio da Fabriano's voice at the Council of Trent urging that creative minds reproduce to the fullest detail the horrors of martydom, Tasso's literary or artistic principle that the piled-up representation of Baroque, "le beau désordre," is contained in an essential unity ("diversi aspetti in un confusi e misti").[64] A compilation of critical passages or texts dating from 1560-1660 which might be gathered together to form a patchwork poetics for Baroque has yet to be undertaken.

The reader has by now been struck by the obvious fact that literary and aesthetic theory of the humanistic period flourished

62. Wylie Sypher, *Four Stages of Renaissance Style* (New York, 1955), p. 238.

63. Helmut Hatzfeld, "A Clarification of the Baroque Problem in the Romance Literatures," *Comparative Literature*, I (1949), 128-29.

64. Tasso, *Gerusalemme liberata*, iv, 5.

especially in Italy. Our peregrine muse carried a baggage of theory and criticism along with her. If it is now recognized that Du Bellay, considered for many years the most vigorous and original theorizer of France, owes an enormous debt to Sperone Speroni, similarly one must recognize the dominion of Italian thought over the discussions of art throughout Europe. Italy occupied the post of honor as cradle of the third classicism. The Europeans accepted the superiority of classical theory reworked by the Italians, and even Albrecht Dürer made his pilgrimage to Italy, like all the rest. The same held true for Italian techniques and practices. Thus Michelangelo could state almost without chauvinism, "If by a miracle someone who is not Italian should succeed in painting well, then, even if he were not consciously imitating Italy, one would say that he painted like an Italian."[65] Similarly, the wanderings of our Italian muse errant (of whom Budé complained in his *De Asse*) left the poets of France, Spain, and England copying Petrarch, adapting the plots of the *novelle,* working the genres formulated by Italy, and repeating and honoring the precepts of Aristotle as they had read them in the Latin or Italian versions by Segni, Robortelli, Castelvetro, and others. It is striking that these countries which boasted of such individual geniuses as Shakespeare, Rabelais, and Cervantes, who rise even above their Italian masters, remained completely derivative in the field of aesthetics and criticism. This corollary then exists: where literature was the richest and most chronologically precocious, literary theory was the richest, while art theory turned out to be more developed and sustained where the fine arts themselves were most advanced.

It was stated earlier that one branch of Renaissance literature, emblem literature, could well illustrate how widespread was the recurrence of the Horatian phrase and notion of *ut pictura poesis.* Certainly the identity of purpose and of intention of arts and letters was especially understood by authors of the emblem books, those volumes of essays and poetry illustrated with engravings of wood or metal. The popularity of these books was so great during the Renaissance that there were issued in the sixteenth century more editions of Andrea Alciati than of Rabelais. These authors of the little-literature, a literature appreciated even by the illiterate, reminded their readers dutifully that, according to Plutarch, Simonides had called pictures silent poetry and poems silent pictures. The emblematists, who used their plates and their

---

65. Francisco de Hollanda, *Dialogos, ed. cit.,* pp. 190-91.

texts as mutual accessories, complementing each other, were almost automatically interested in the parallels between poetry or prose and the fine or graphic arts. One book of emblems which appeared in 1552 bore the significant title, *Picta Poesis, ut Pictura Poesis erit*.[66] Christophorus Giarda, repeating the definitions of Simonides, writes extensively in his *Icones symbolicae* on the relations between pen and brush. Poetry, he says, is an emulatory picture of nature. Painters, seeing how perfectly poets imitate nature and how much praise they win, set out to surpass them. So painters descend into the arena as once did Zeuxis and Parrhasius. Giarda's development of this theme, evoking Plato and Horace, insists on the equality of the sister arts and vituperates those who would set up a quarrel between them:

sed meum non est litem hanc inter sorores componere. Illud quidem non abs re mea existimo, ab illa, quae ambas inter reperitur, similitudine probare, poesim esse picturam loquentem, picturam vero tacitam poesim.[67]

When Gomberville, another emblematist, explains what he reads into one of the emblems of the Dutchman Otto Vaenius, he qualifies, "Si j'entends bien son langage muet."[68]

A last illustration of the *pictura poesis* might be quoted from emblem literature. It is the fourth volume of the famous *Icones virorum illustrium* of Boissard, where the author relates the myth of Vulcan, Mars, and Venus—a favorite theme of painters up to Rubens—and explains its symbolism. He adds that the ancients had entertained themselves with such themes, whether pictorially or poetically. We must discover and understand the allegory of such themes, wherever we find them, in books or on canvas. The allegorical sense is a challenge in either case.

Hisce et similibus fabulamentis antiquitas plurimum oblectata fuit, sunt enim res poeticae et quaedam picturae, ut pictura poesis, erit, . . . item pictoribus atque poetis, . . . at ex rebus pictis et fictis sensa eligere, hoc est sapientis opus.[69]

These writers of emblem books were less important arbiters than a Scaliger, a Ronsard, a Vives, or a Sidney. But they were so sensitive to the taste of the greatest masses that we have in their production a precious cross-section of the bourgeois and proletarian thought of the Renaissance. The reappearance of

66. Barthélemy Aneau, *Picta Poesis, ut Pictura Poesis erit* (Lyon, 1552).
67. Christophorus Giarda, *Icones symbolicae* (Milan, 1628), p. 96.
68. Le Roy de Gomberville, *Le Théâtre moral de la vie humaine* (Brussels, 1678), p. 126.
69. Lebey de Batilly, *Icones virorum illustrium* (Frankfurt, 1597-99) IV, 3ᵛ.

the *ut pictura poesis* in these emblemata is the best possible evidence of the horizontal and vertical extension of this Horatian notion and its deformations in the late humanistic period.

Before we leave the rich and suggestive subject matter of this essay it might be interesting to explore how the *ut pictura poesis* parallel operated when artist and poet coincided in a single man. Would there not be in such a case multiple interrelations of every type? The best example of this dual personality was perhaps the "gymnosophist" Michelangelo Buonarroti, hailed at his death as *trismegistos*, outstanding in painting, sculpture, and verse. Holding the conviction that God or nature plants preconceived forms in the *hyle*, the raw material of art (stone, marble, clay, iron, gold, wax), Michelangelo applies his theory of the *concetto* to poetry as well, and affirms to Tommaso Cavalieri that high and low styles are prefigured in ink just as form lies waiting within marble.[70] In the *Dialogos em Roma*, recorded by his friend the Portuguese miniaturist De Hollanda (See Chapter VI of this volume), Michelangelo says that Dame Painting was during antiquity the sovereign of all writers and historians.[71] During these colloquies Buonarroti shows himself more liberal than Horace in declaring the parallel rights of poets and painters to give free rein to their fantasy.

In modern times it has become a familiar exercise to underscore the points of contact and parallels between the *Rime* and the art of Michelangelo. One of the first to do so was the unhappy Ugo Foscolo, presenting and explaining the *canzoniere* of Michelangelo to his English hosts in 1826. Foscolo observes that the often-rough poetic style of Michelangelo was consonant with the rough appearance of some of his unfinished statuary. Some of the poems were even *non finiti*, abandoned just as Michelangelo abandoned the statues in which he felt himself incapable of capturing the basic form, the *concetto*. If he took delight in drawing forth a figure from the confining dimensions of a block of marble, he took no less pleasure working in the compressing and compressed form of the sonnet. Nesca Robb writes, "It was left for Michelangelo to inform the Petrarchan-Neoplatonic lyric with something of the fire and vigor that distinguishes his art."[72] Valerio Mariani finds in the epigrammatic

---

70. Carl Frey, *Die Dichtungen*, *ed. cit.*, p. 54.
71. Francisco de Hollanda, *Dialogos*, *ed. cit.*, p. 208.
72. Nesca Robb, *Neoplatonism of the Italian Renaissance* (London, 1935), p. 240.

and meditative poetry composed on the occasion of the death of young Cecchino de' Bracci a conscious attempt at marmoreal and lapidary expression. The continuous use by Michelangelo of images, metaphors, and expressions reveals a poet subject to plasticizing tendencies and a desire to exploit the mimetic similarities of art and poetry. Mariani picks from Michelangelo's poetry not only many plastic metaphors, but many terms derived from the fine arts: "pietra, sasso, scoglio, marmo, intaglio, martello, ferro, ruina, scorza," and a "hammering recourse to harsh and metallic sounds."[73] "His poetic expression is converted into a keen chiseling in hard materials and the crudity of certain words approximates many parts of his statuary left scarcely indicated, so that as a contrast the effect of those verses that he tirelessly spins and elaborates may result in a finer facture."

It is clear that Michelangelo sought to avail himself of the communicability of the fine arts to bear the same messages as his writings. Thus, De Tolnay notes that the first *pensiero* (version) of his *Venus and Cupid* represents that goddess in the act of warding off the infant Amor and establishes an analogy with the poem of Michelangelo, "Fuggite, Amanti, amor, fuggite 'l foco; l'incendio è aspro, e la piaga è mortale."[74] The *Cristo risorto* of Michelangelo and more especially his *Cristo giudice* on the wall of the Sistine are "mute poesies" corresponding to his verses which complain of the moral dissolution of Rome, where the blood of Christ is sold by the bucketful ("Quasi fa elmi di calici e spade").

At times Michelangelo's artistic creations were to retell the messages of other writers, as Lomazzo had suggested. Primary and secondary sources of his art have been encountered in works of literature and philosophy—among others, the *Cratylus*, the *Phaedo*, the Old and New Testaments, the hymns of Saint Ambrose, Dante, Petrarch, Villani, Guicciardini, Poliziano, Ficino, Sannazaro, Savonarola. For example, the *Fetonte* of Michelangelo follows closely the text of Ovid's *Metamorphoses*.

These *obiter dicta,* which make up a brief parenthetical aside, show in a fragmentary way how one may pursue the study of the *ut pictura poesis* in the life of a single artist or writer of the Renaissance.

One final, basic parallel must be established between the art treatises and the poetic tracts. This concerns the lasting value of

73. Valerio Mariani, *La Poesia di Michelangelo* (Rome, 1941), p. 135.
74. Charles de Tolnay, *The Medici Chapel* (Princeton, 1948), p. 108.

all the above-mentioned Renaissance thinking, as contrasted with the "invention" of aesthetics by Baumgarten, Winckelmann, Hume, Lessing, Du Bos, and others in the eighteenth century. The Renaissance did not merely rediscover ancient works of art and literature. It derived new canons of beauty and form from the works which it inherited and which in so many cases had been there to examine all along. This undertaking was an operation in "aesthetics." Stripped of their self-contained and metaphysical vocabulary, the issues found in the treatises of Baumgarten and his contemporaries are those which we have enumerated above as chief preoccupations of the humanistic *ars poetica* and *ars pictoria.* Although the Renaissance theorists on art and letters did not possess such a broad historical perspective as their successors, their speculations thought things out in as thorough and original and consistent a fashion as did those of their successors, and frequently with as strict a vocabulary of key words and concepts. Our investigation of the Renaissance *artes* helps us to understand that in the full humanistic aesthetic, barriers between the branches of creative endeavor may be disregarded. And long before Ben Jonson and Dryden, not to mention Croce or the regretted Menéndez y Pelayo, all arts of the spirit may be viewed as a single entity, within the great collective impulse conveyed by the Greek word *poiésis.*

II

RILKE, MICHELANGELO, AND THE
GESCHICHTEN VOM LIEBEN GOTT

A FULL assessment of the spirit which infuses Rilke's thirteen *Geschichten vom lieben Gott* has never been undertaken. In fact, the copious studies, essays, and memoirs which caused Gide to observe, as far back as February 1927, "Tout a été dit sur Rainer Maria Rilke," have been less concerned with these somewhat enigmatic tales than with the other works. Despite the fact that they were written on seven successive nights in a single sustained impulse, they are not entirely homogeneous in spirit. Certainly, harmony is lent throughout by the reappearance of a gentle, anthropomorphic God of an enlightened sort who is baffled by that comportment of mankind which baffles the narrator himself. The successive titles of this collection announced God as a unifying force ("Du, mein Gott, wer sonst!"). Yet within this general and harmonizing spirit there is heterogeneity provided by "seltsame, oft bizarr wirkende Vergleiche und Bilder"[1] which seem capricious inventions and reminiscences. It is our intention to identify the spirit and source of many of these passages. This spirit, implicit from the very first legend and finally explicit in the eighth, is that of Michelangelo Buonarroti.

Two contrary formative forces operated on the composition of the *Geschichten* in November 1899, the same forces apparent in *Vom mönchischen Leben*, dating from the same season and year. Between late March and early May 1898, Rilke made his first trip to Florence via Arco and Viareggio; he had been to Venice in the spring of the previous year. In April, May, and June of 1899 he made his first trip to Moscow, a trip which he felt would bring new depths of religiosity to his writing, as he wrote to Frieda von Bülow, and one which would complement his stay in Florence.[2] It was at the very moment when, with Lou Andreas-Salomé, he was reconciling and synthesizing his intensive study of Russia and Russian with his specific study of the Italian Renaissance and when the memories of his two recent trips were freshest that Rilke wrote these "children's stories." Three of them were actually set in Russia and three in Italy.

1. Albert Schäfer, *Die Gottesanschauung Rainer Maria Rilkes* (Würzburg, 1938), p. 38.
2. Rilke, *Briefe und Tagebücher aus der Frühzeit* (Leipzig, 1931), p. 16.

The trip to Florence—to the Cappella Medicea, the Bargello, the Casa Buonarroti, and the rest—brought Rilke face to face with the plastic works of Michelangelo. His description of the *Deposizione* in the Duomo (which he, like his contemporaries, called the *Pietà*) as a *non finito* in "Von einem, der die Steine belauscht" came out of personal observation, as did his awareness of Michelangelo's absorption in the nude figure. Yet, as attested by the *rapprochements* we shall identify in the *Geschichten*, it was less the marbles, canvases, and frescoes of Michelangelo which absorbed Rilke in 1899 than the mind and temperament of the Florentine artist as revealed in his writings and recorded statements. For in those writings, particularly the *Rime* and the *Lettere*, Rilke found a fascinating fellow craftsman whose passionate temperament, whose unbending devotion to his art, and whose Christian-Platonic mysticism transcending penury and misunderstanding all struck a responsive chord in his own troubled being. Yet, of all the scholars and dilettantes represented in Walter Ritzer's *Rilke Bibliographie*, none has explored the ascendancy of Buonarroti over René Rilke.

In 1899, for the first time, it was possible for Rilke to have the five major sources for Michelangelo's thought at his disposal in readily available editions, editions which have never been superseded. That year, moreover, initiated a period when it was almost impossible for a young intellectual in Germany or Austria, especially if he had a reading knowledge of Italian, to avoid becoming acquainted with Michelangelo. In 1899 a generous *Sammlung* of letters to Michelangelo was brought out in Berlin by Carl Frey. The monumental Milanesi edition of the artist's letters had been available since 1875. The final volume of Milanesi's edition of Vasari's *Vite* had appeared in 1882, and in 1887 Frey reissued in Berlin the biographies of Michelangelo by Vasari and Condivi. In 1897 Frey published in Berlin his definitive *Dichtungen des Michelagniolo Buonarroti*, whose readings were to be used later by Rilke in his own *Dichtungen des Michelangelo*. It should be added parenthetically that in 1899 the few extant German translations of Michelangelo were disparaged knowingly by Rilke as "ein Spiel kindischer Reimereien."[3] He excepted from this condemnation only the few pieces which had been translated by Hermann Grimm, like Frey a professor of art at the University of Berlin. Granted the opportune appearance of these four sources, the *Rime*, the *Lettere*, and the

3. Rilke, *Briefe* (Wiesbaden, 1950), II, 292.

Vite of Vasari and of Condivi, what access did Rilke have to the fifth major reservoir of Buonarrotian thought, those dialogues in which Francisco de Hollanda recorded so many of Michelangelo's pronouncements on art? On the eve of the composition of the *Geschichten,* Vasconcellos published in Vienna De Hollanda's *Vier Gespräche über die Malerei* (1899) with facing German and Portuguese texts.

Rilke evidently preferred to use the Italian versions of the sources that were also available in German. One gathers this from his statement to Lou Andreas-Salomé that he knew only the Italian text of the *Rime,*[4] and the supposition is unexpectedly confirmed in two verses of the first part of the *Stundenbuch,* also dating from late 1899:

> Das waren Tage Michelangelos
> Von denen ich in fremden Büchern las.[5]

Further evidence that Rilke was using these primary sources rather than Grimm's popular biography of Michelangelo, which reproduces fragments of the letters and the *Rime,* is supplied by a recently published letter of Rilke to Graf Mensdorff under date of January 1, 1917: ". . . das schönste grundlegende Buch, das sein Leben erzählt, ist sicher das von Hermann Grimm, das Ihnen dringend empfohlen sei, das ich aber selbst leider nie gelesen habe. Die grosse italiänische Ausgabe der Gedichte, nach der ich übersetze, enthält einen ziemlich grossen Apparat von Anmerkungen, mit dem ich mir helfe. . . ." This could be only the edition of Frey. The letter quoted is reproduced in *Mesa,* IV (Spring 1952), 25-26, and was brought to my attention by my friend Professor Philip Shelley. These sources, all of them recently available to him and the vehicles of a Michelangelo revival, are reflected in varying degrees in several of the *Geschichten vom lieben Gott.*

Perhaps still conscious of Michelangelo at that moment when he set down his pen, exhausted as though he had been wielding a chisel and mallet, Rilke signaled in his *Tagebuch* the completion of the "Buch vom lieben Gott und Anderes" with a free-verse acknowledgment of the divine forces which had buoyed him up night after night:

---

4. Rilke, *Briefe* (Leipzig, 1933), III, 190.
5. Rilke, *Gesammelte Werke* (Leipzig, 1927), II, 193.

die nicht von meiner müden Hand sind. Die
verraten, dass ich selber Hand bin, Eines,
der mit mir wundersame Dinge tut.[6]

It is the same acknowledgment which Michelangelo on several
occasions makes to the God who guides his hand. On one of these
occasions he expressed himself in a sonnet which Rilke was shortly to translate:

se 'l mie rozzo martello i duri sassi
Forma d'uman aspecto or questo or quello,
Dal ministro, che 'l guida iscorgie e tiello,
prendendo il moto, ua con gli altrui passi.[7]

Wenn hier mein grober Hammer den und den
härtesten Stein in Menschenhaftes wandel,
hat er den Schwung von dem, der mit ihm handelt
und muss mit eines andern Schritten gehn.[8]

God as the *sommo fattore,* the actual force behind the "pronta
mano" of the artist is an idea conveyed *passim* in Michelangelo's
writings.[9]

If the spirit of Botticelli infuses many of the early *Mädchen-
bilder,* it is Michelangelo who is evoked directly or indirectly in
six of the tales of God.

In the first tale, "Das Märchen von den Händen Gottes,"
the narrator announces at the outset that he knows something
about these hands. Indeed, they were a prominent motif throughout *Vom mönchischen Leben,* completed a few weeks earlier.
Rilke leads us up to the subject as though he were enumerating
the first histories of the Sistine Ceiling preceding the *Creazione
di Adamo:* "Also der liebe Gott begann, wie bekannt, seine Arbeit, indem er die Erde machte, diese vom Wasser unterschied,
und Licht befahl."[10] The rapidity of this creating ("in bewun-
dernswerter Geschwindigkeit") impresses Rilke, as it impressed
Michelangelo in his sonnet, "Colui che fece et non di cosa alcuna"
(in Rilke's *Dichtungen* this becomes "Der, welcher, nicht aus
irgend einem Dinge").[11] Rilke explains that this rapidity is possible only after long and deep planning; everything must be

6. Rilke, *Briefe und Tagebücher aus der Frühzeit* (Leipzig, 1931), p. 231.
7. Carl Frey, ed., *Dichtungen des Michelagniolo Buonarroti* (Berlin, 1897),
p. 106.
8. Rilke, *Dichtungen des Michelangelo* (Wiesbaden, 1951), p. 42.
9. Frey, *Dichtungen,* pp. 4, 228, and *passim.*
10. Rilke, *Geschichten vom lieben Gott* (Leipzig, 1936), p. 11.
11. Frey, *Dichtungen,* p. 4; Rilke, *Dichtungen,* p. 32.

ready in the head before the hand can execute. This is a basic
tenet of Michelangelo, who held that the mind must resolve
the problem of the *concetto* with deliberation, so that the final
operation may be (and appear to be) rapid and effortless. This
Michelangelo confided to Francisco de Hollanda as a crucial trade
secret: "Was man mit grösstem Eifer erstreben und mit dem
grössten Aufwand von Arbeit und Studium, im Schweisse seines
Angesichts zu erreichen suchen soll, ist dasjenige, dass, was man
mit allergrösster Mühe schafft, so aussehe, als wäre es schnell,
fast ohne Anstrengung, ja mit grösster Leichtigkeit hingewor-
fen."[12]

God is completely indifferent to external nature and takes no
interest in creating trees. His disdain is reminiscent of Michelangelo's, as explained by Vasari in a well-known passage: "Ha
Michelagnolo atteso solo, comme s'è detto altrove, alla perfezione
dell'arte; perchè nè paesi vi sono, nè alberi . . . come quegli
che forse non voleva abbassare quel suo grande ingegno in simil
cose."[13] When God starts to make animals, He grows more interested; but He becomes completely absorbed in the making
of man. The lack of interest in trees and animals is translated
into the first histories of the Sistine Ceiling. Angels flutter
around God, capable of fright, like the *putti* on the Sistine *Crea-
zioni*. God turns the completion of the sculpturing of man over
to His hands, and sight is no longer an agent of the formative
process.[14] We are thus guided to the *Creazione di Adamo*, where
the hands impart life to man. The distinct functions of the mind
and the hands were explicit in Michelangelo: "le mani operano
e l'occhio giudica."[15] Man, however, slips out of God's hands
and falls—the theme of three of the remaining five panels. God
thereupon disowns His hands and even today, unless the hands
have the succor of God, they are as powerless as art without
nature. "Ohne Gott gibt es keine Vollendung."[16] This is a lesson

12. De Hollanda, *Vier Gespräche über die Malerei* (Vienna, 1899), p. 121.

13. Vasari, *Le Vite* (Florence, 1881), VII, 216.

14. *Geschichten*, p. 15. Are these detached hands of independent will, to be
exploited so fully by Cocteau, part of that unspecified debt which Cocteau acknowledged to "le secrétaire de M. Rodin"? (And does his *angélisme* derive
from the angelism of Rilke?)

15. Vasari, *Le Vite*, VII, 270.

16. *Geschichten*, p. 16. The idea that God is needed for the completion of
man's works had recently been introduced in the *Stundenbuch*, where the efforts
of the "Knappen, Jünger, Meister" require the final collaboration of God:
"Aber wer kann dich vollenden, du Dom . . . ?" *Gesammelte Werke*, II, 191,
184.

Michelangelo will learn bitterly in the eighth tale. The notion of the hands proving inadequate to the task when the mind is inattentive was enunciated by Michelangelo: "e' non si può lavorare con le mani una cosa, e col ciervello una altra," or again, "si dipinge col ciervello e non con le mani."[17]

At this point Rilke proceeds to one of the dominant ideas of Michelangelo's aesthetics—the supremacy of the nude over the clothed figure. After a moment of eternity (a thousand calendar years) God looks down and sees a great milling throng of over a million. "Aber sie waren alle schon in Kleidern . . . so bekam Gott einen ganz falschen und sehr schlechten Begriff von den Menschen." Michelangelo's specific condemnation of clothing Rilke may have found in the newly published *Vier Gespräche:* "Wo aber ist ein Verstand so stumpfsinnig, dass er nicht begriffe, dass ein Menschenfuss edler ist als ein Schuh? Und die menschliche Haut schöner als ein Lammfell, mit dem man jene etwa bekleidet?"[18] Fortunately, there are a few people left in the world to remind God of the beauty of the nude figure: "Einfach die Kinder und dann und wann auch diejenigen Leute, welche malen, Gedichte schreiben, bauen," three pursuits in which Michelangelo distinguished himself. Various of Buonarroti's *Rime* ("Mentre c'alla belta, ch'i' uiddi im prima," "Veggio nel tuo bel uiso, Signior mio," "Per ritornar la donde uenne fora") propagate the Neoplatonic belief that the human body constitutes one of three levels at which God is mirrored, the supreme perfection of form, and a visible manifestation of "quel pietoso fonte, onde siam tucti" ("Gnadenquell, aus welchem alle stammen").[19]

This exaltation of the nude figure furnished the answer to the question implicit in the title of the third tale, "Warum der liebe Gott will, dass es arme Leute gibt." God continues to regret that man clothes himself so fully that He can no longer see what man is like. The loss of the contours of the body within the clothing ("dass man sah, es konnte kein Körper mehr darunter sein")[20] which God regrets was equally intolerable to Michelangelo. The most perfect example of his rebellion against raiment was one which Rilke had recently observed—the figure of Giuliano de' Medici, with the transparent coat of mail.

17. *Le Lettere di Michelangelo Buonarroti,* ed. Milanesi (Florence, 1875), pp. 450, 489.
18. De Hollanda, *Vier Gespräche,* p. 117.
19. Frey, *Dichtungen,* p. 53; Rilke, *Dichtungen,* p. 40.
20. *Geschichten,* p. 39.

The principal episode of this third tale concerns the erection of a nude statue of Truth in a public square. God finds the modeler of this statue, an irritable man, kneading clay and complaining that he should never have become an artist: "Ich wollte, ich wär Schuster geworden. Da sitzt man und plagt sich."[21] His complaint is a paraphrase of Michelangelo's outcry in a letter: "Meglio m'era nei primi anni che io mi fussi messo a fare zolfanelli che io non sarei in tanta passione."[22] At this point the reminiscence of Michelangelo becomes most keen. The iracund sculptor (and testimony abounds concerning the short temper of Michelangelo) works day and night to execute his allegorical figure, only to have the city fathers and other eminences decide that the pudenda should be covered. This scandalized reaction is a vivid evocation of Michelangelo's struggle to protect his nude figures from *braghettoni*—from dignitaries of the Church and Counter-Reformational bodies down to the vulgar Aretino, who wrote a "lettre de Tartuffe" (Romain Rolland's phrase) charging that the figures of the Sistine Chapel would be more fitting to a bordello. "Der liebe Gott verstand nicht, weshalb, so laut fluchte der Künstler." Loud indeed was Buonarroti's first reaction when he was told to his astonishment and irritation that the Pope wanted to put loincloths on the nudities of the *Giudizio universale:* "Dite al papa che questa è piccola faccenda, e che facilmente si può acconciare; che acconci egli il mondo!"[23] The thematic proposition that the poor and unclothed are the most virtuous people and the most beloved of God reminds one of a passage in Vasari. When Pope Julius found the Sistine ceiling "poor," Michelangelo retorted that primitive men and religious men could indeed appear plain and bare. "Padre Santo, in quel tempo gli uomini non portavano addosso oro, e quegli che son dipinti non furon mai troppo ricchi, ma santi uomini, perchè gli sprezzarono le ricchezze."[24]

The slim little tale draws quickly to a close. The schoolmaster, to whom it is being narrated, fails to understand this enlightened approach to Biblical materials and objects: "Zunächst finde ich es unrecht, religiöse, besonders biblische Stoffe frei und eigenmächtig zu gebrauchen." This is the very complaint which Gilio da Fabriano, one of the loudest mouthpieces of the Counter-

21. *Ibid.*
22. Milanesi, *Lettere*, p. 488.
23. Vasari, *Le Vite*, VII, 240.
24. *Ibid.*, VII, 178.

Reformation, lodged against Michelangelo's paintings, and which was to have its echoes, incidentally, in the charges against Paolo Veronese before the Holy Tribunal and in the *Procesos inquisitoriales contra Francisco Sánchez de las Brozas*. It is a counterpart of the feeling of Rilke's monk, in an unpublished passage of the *Stundenbuch*, that Michelangelo and his fellows were blasphemous in their endeavor to represent God.[25]

The titular hero of the eighth tale, "Von einem, der die Steine belauscht," is Michelangelo. This tripartite story is composed of three episodes in the life of the artist, two adapted from Vasari and all three growing out of an intimate understanding of Michelangelo's personal aesthetics, based on the *concetto* as a predetermined, living, and growing art form.

At the outset the narrator returns to the theme of anthropocentrism introduced in the first tale. God is much less interested in external nature than in man. "Der Frühling, den Gott bemerken soll, darf nicht in Bäumen auf Wiesen bleiben, er muss irgendwie in den Menschen mächtig werden."[26] We have already observed that this attitude of the master sculptor was that of Buonarroti, who advised Vasari to use nude figures rather than *fogliami* as decorative motifs.[27] Michelangelo's preference for nude figures in a "terra inanis et vacua" leads him to censure the Flemings for painting "patches, masonries, plants in the fields, shadows of trees, rivers, and bridges, all of which they call landscapes."[28] Like the Aristotelian theorists of his time, Michelangelo saw "man in action" (or "under tension") as the only valid subject of painting and sculpture as well as of tragedy and epic.

In a baroque setting God and the angels hover over Renaissance Italy and watch the restless hands of Michelangelo—at first seemingly folded as if in prayer ("aber das Gebet, welches ihnen entquoll, drängte sie weit auseinander")—cast a shadow over the peninsula. God does not resent this shadow. Indeed, He disregards the prayers of others which rise up heavenward to Him, and views Michelangelo's creative power as an offering to Him. The real-life Michelangelo did indeed feel that his exercise of painting, sculpture, and architecture was a service

25. See Ruth Mövius, *Rainer Maria Rilkes Stundenbuch* (Leipzig, 1937), pp. 209-15.
26. *Geschichten*, p. 101.
27. Vasari, *Le Vite*, VII, 226.
28. De Hollanda, *Vier Gespräche*, p. 29.

dedicated to God.[29] God then looks more closely over the shoulder of the craftsman. He observes that the hands seem to be listening to the stone they are working and gives a start. Do the stones themselves have souls? Apparently hearing a faint voice from the stone, the hands set again to fashioning it.

A major premise of Michelangelo's Neoplatonism was that art forms co-exist in the world of soul and the world of matter. It fostered his belief that living figures were sealed within marbles ("gardiens du contour pur"), a belief expressed in several poems known to Rilke, as his *Dichtungen* show:

> Si come per leuar, Donna, si pone
> In pietra alpestra e dura
> Una uiua figura,
> Che là piu crescie, u' piu la pietra scema.[30]

> So wie, indem man abnimmt, langsam nur
> innen im harten Berggestein sich findet
> ein Niederschlag lebendiger Figur,
> der mehr erwächst, je mehr der Stein verschwindet.[31]

Once it is accepted that the living *concetto* in the stone has a soul, it is easy to attribute a voice to it. This element of Michelangelo's thinking was so apparent to Rilke that he translated all three poems which are allegedly spoken by the living marbles. These are the stanza spoken by the *Notte* of the Medici Chapel, the dialogue between the *Giorno* and the *Notte*, and the plaint of the headstone on the sepulcher of Cecchino de' Bracci:

> Caro m'è 'l sonno et piu l'esser di sasso[32]
> Schlaf ist mir lieb, doch über alles preise[33]

> El Di e la Nocte parlano e dichono[34]
> Es sprechen der Tag und die Nacht und sagen[35]

> Dagli alti monti e d'una gra' ruina[36]
> Von Bergen, wo der Felsen im Verein[37]

---

29. Thus, when Michelangelo became architect-in-chief of St. Peter's, he refused an extra emolument from Paul III, stating that he was agreeing to serve in this new role only for his love of God.

30. Frey, *Dichtungen*, p. 90.

31. Rilke, *Dichtungen*, p. 7.

32. Frey, *Dichtungen*, p. 126.

33. Rilke, *Dichtungen*, p. 5.

34. Frey, *Dichtungen*, p. 14.

35. Rilke, *Gesammelte Werke*, VI, 225. Omitted in the Insel edition of *Dichtungen des Michelangelo*.

36. Frey, *Dichtungen*, p. 222.

37. Rilke, *Dichtungen*, p. 60.

God, still startled by the faint voice in the stone, cries out: "Michelangelo, wer ist im Stein?" The answer comes up, "Du, mein Gott, wer denn sonst. Aber ich kann nicht zu dir."

The idea of Michelangelo's trying to attain God can be read in many of the *Rime* which Rilke put into German. God's unattainability for Michelangelo had occupied Rilke a few weeks before, while writing *Vom mönchischen Leben:*

> Nur Gott bleibt über seinem Willen weit:
> da liebt er ihn seinem hohen Hasse
> für diese Unerreichbarkeit.[38]

After Michelangelo has answered that God Himself is in the stone, the Deity becomes conscious of this, in a passage which could have been written only by someone familiar with Michelangelo's *concetto* theory:

> Und da fühlte Gott, dass er auch im Steine sei, und es wurde ihm ängstlich und enge. Der ganze Himmel war nur ein Stein, und er war mitten drin eingeschlossen und hoffte auf die Hände Michelangelos, die ihn befreien würden, und er hörte sie kommen, aber noch weit.[39]

If God is a conception to be created by masters and apprentices, as Rilke had written in the first part of the *Stundenbuch*,[40] it is meet that he should be freed (formed) by the sculptor laureate of Christendom.

The narrator shifts to the viewpoint of the sculptor, whose attention is now riveted upon a marble block in which his inner vision discerns the three figures of the *Deposizione* in the Florentine Duomo. It is no accident that Rilke selects this particular work to lend unity to his tale. For it is the one work in which both God and Michelangelo are incarnated, in the figures of Christ and Nicodemus, respectively. It serves as a transitional element between the concepts of God as a marmoreal art form, just introduced, and of Michelangelo as a similar art form, which closes the tale. That Nicodemus was a self-portrait, by the way, was known as far back as Vasari, and any native of Florence will assure you of the fact today. Seeing the three figures *in potenza* within the stone, Rilke's Michelangelo self-consciously echoes the most famous quatrain of the *Rime:* "Er dachte beständig : du bist nur ein kleiner Block, und ein anderer könnte in dir kaum einen Mensch finden. . . ."

38. Rilke, *Gesammelte Werke,* II, 194.
39. *Geschichten,* p. 103.
40. Rilke, *Gesammelte Werke,* II, 191.

Non ha l'ottimo artista alcun concetto,
Ch' un marmo solo in se non circonscriua
Col suo souerchio, et solo à quello arriua
La man, che ubbidisce all'intelletto.[41]

Then this recreated Michelangelo goes further than his archetype had ever gone, wondering why he may not lift an entire
sleeping race out of a rock. In a sense, the painter of the Sistine
frescoes, including the *Giudizio*, who applied this theory of the
predetermined *concetto* to painting,[42] did bring an entire race out
of the pigment which had enclosed them. In any case, Rilke's
sculptor "sets free" the figures of the *Deposizione* with "broad
strokes," the same broad strokes which impressed Cellini as the
result of the "awesome furies which came over him as he worked."[43] But the surfaces of the *Deposizione* are purposely kept
indistinct: "er löste nicht ganz die steinernen Schleier von ihren
Gesichtern, als fürchtete er, ihre tiefe Traurigkeit könnte sich
lähmend über seine Hände legen." This expedient of the stone
veil to soften the outright depiction of pain is as old as the Greek
artist who left a statue of Agamemnon unfinished, fearing his
inability to translate the anguish of a father seeing his daughter
sacrificed; in any case, Michelangelo's contemporaries Lomazzo
and Dolce both mention his recourse to the "veil of art."[44]

Michelangelo thereupon turns to other stones, and does not
complete the figures which he finds in them. They would be
most likely the *San Matteo*, the *Giorno*, and the *Prigioni*, all of
which Rilke had undoubtedly seen in Florence. Rilke is now
posing the problem of the *non finiti*, a problem which has troubled
and attracted many art historians. Rilke offers his own explanation, advanced by no one else. Michelangelo does not finish a
statue, "damit ihre Schönheit nicht ganz verraten sei."

The narrator now turns his attention to a well-known occasion
in 1505 when Michelangelo was overseeing the quarrying of
marbles at Carrara, seeking suitable blocks for the ill-fated
tomb of Julius II.[45] He will cover the tomb with a "Geschlecht"

41. Frey, *Dichtungen*, p. 89.

42. Michelangelo even applied this theory to writing and poetry, finding
style resident in the ink itself, in a sonnet ("Sicome nella penna e nell'
inchiostro") translated by Rilke ("So wie drei Stile in der Feder sind").

43. Cellini, *Due trattati* (Milan, 1811), p. 213.

44. Lomazzo, *Trattato di pittura e scultura* (Rome, 1844), I, 47; Dolce,
Dialogo della pittura (Florence, 1735), p. 242.

45. See Vasari, *Le Vite*, VII, 163; and Condivi, *Vita di Michelangiolo* (Florence, 1938), p. 61.

of figures, obviously the many allegorical Victories, Captives, and so on. As Vasari and Condivi indicate, the master's eye fastens upon a high mountain peak within which his mind's eye seems to see a colossus taking form. As the image of the colossus grows, the initial impression of the mountain dies away: "Und Michelangelo fühlte seine Gestalt wachsen unter dem Einfluss dieses Blickes."

> L'inmagin dentro crescie, e quella cede
> Quasi uilmente e senza alcuna stima.[46]

Soon the sculptor feels that he, too, is growing in stature, just as Buonarroti was pictured as waxing "gigantengross" in the *Stundenbuch*.[47] He looks down and sees the huts underfoot far below, like that giant described by Michelangelo:

> Vn gigante u'è ancor d'alteza tanta,
> Che da sua ochi noi qua giu non uede . . .
> Al sol aspira e l'alte torre pianta. . . .[48]

> Ein Riese ist noch, über alles gross,
> uns unten hier sehn seine Augen nicht . . .
> Zur Sonne lässt er seine Türme los. . . .[49]

Then Rilke knowledgeably describes the *furia* of Michelangelo's figures in a few well-chosen words. Of the colossus Michelangelo perceives in the mountain peak, he writes: "Es hatte einen wartenden Ausdruck, reglos und doch am Rande der Bewegung."[50] This is the renowned action-in-check of Buonarroti's statuary and painting, achieved through a carefully contrived exploitation of contrapposto and serpentine, on which he expressed himself to Marco da Siena.[51] Gratified at the indestructible unity promised by such a colossal statue, Michelangelo decides to accept the challenge of executing it ("Dich will ich vollenden") and turns back toward Florence, which in this fairy tale lies just around the corner. But God does not will it, and we have been forewarned in the first tale that "ohne Gott gibt es keine Vollendung."

That this memorable incident in Michelangelo's biography was lingering in Rilke's mind when he composed the first part of the *Stundenbuch* a few weeks before may be assumed from the poet's outcry to God therein:

46. Frey, *Dichtungen*, p. 24.
47. Rilke, *Gesammelte Werke*, II, 193.
48. Frey, *Dichtungen*, p. 58.
49. Rilke, *Dichtungen*, p. 66.
50. *Geschichten*, p. 105.
51. Lomazzo, *Trattato*, I, 34-35; II, 87.

und hätt dich gebildet, wie ein Gigant
dich bilden würde: als Berg. . . .[52]

As Buonarroti enters Florence, he sees a star over the tower
of the Duomo, reminiscent of a legend of the Savonarolians to
the effect that the sculptor saw a comet arched toward Florence.[53]
Then the eighth tale races to a highly imaginative conclusion,
for which we were subtly prepared by the introduction of Nicodemus above. Michelangelo suddenly begins to feel the *soverchio*
(superfluous surrounding matter) of the city of Florence starting
to encase him as he reaches the Porta Romana. The city blocks,
his own house, his narrow room, and then his walls close in on
him: "und es war, als kämpften sie mit seinen Übermassen und
zwängten ihn zurück in die alte, enge Gestalt. Und er duldete
es. Er drückte sich in die Kniee und liess sich formen von ihnen."

At this point God cries out to him, "Michelangelo, wer ist
in dir?" And the artist, now reduced to one of his own *concetti*,
like Nicodemus, answers, "Du, mein Gott, wer denn sonst."
So God indeed must be the life force in artists who are at one
with their creations and has been in them since He wished to have
fashioned the *arca foederis*, the Ark of the Covenant."[54]

For the final Magnificat Rilke's gaze returns to the upper
plane of the baroque stage setting where the limelights had originally been directed: God in triumph, the saints in their mitres and
mantles, the choir of angels and cherubim, "wie mit Krügen voll
glänzenden Quelle unter den dürstenden Sternen umher, und
es war der Himmel kein Ende."[55]

The application of the concept of the sealed-in art form as a
living thing, enlarged to the point of considering God and Michelangelo as both artists and art forms themselves, makes a fanciful
if complex theme for a short story. In the *Rime* Rilke found
Michelangelo identifying various individuals as actual or potential art forms, *concetti*: Vittoria Colonna, Tommaso Cavalieri,
himself. Since Michelangelo had taken a bolder stand than most
Church painters on iconolatry and anthropomorphism, he did obviously view God as an art form. But the God-in-stone was the
final and logical projection of the *concetto* theory whose "Un-
erreichbarkeit" held him, but not Rilke, back.

In turning out thirteen tales in the short span of seven nights,
could Rilke fail to sense Michelangelo's presence throughout?

52. Rilke, *Gesammelte Werke*, II, 188.
53. "Una visione del Buonarroti," *Il Buonarroti*, IV (April, 1866), 103.
54. De Hollanda, *Vier Gespräche*, p. 110.
55. *Geschichten*, p. 106.

That presence is not noticeable in the stories of direct Russian inspiration, "Wie der Verrat nach Russland kam," "Wie der alte Timofei singend starb," "Das Lied von der Gerechtigkeit," and "Der fremde Mann," which were to demonstrate the new religious accents gained from the first trip to Russia. Neither Italy nor Russia figures in "Wie der Fingerhut dazu kam, der liebe Gott zu sein" or "Ein Märchen vom Tod." Appropriately enough, "Eine Szene aus dem Ghetto von Venedig" evokes Giorgione, Titian, and Tiepolo; there is no evocation of Michelangelo to remind us that it was in this ghetto that the Florentine stayed, to the consternation of the proper Venetians, when he first visited Venice.

Yet in that week of creation in November 1899 momentary snatches of his reading in Michelangelo returned. So, in "Der Bettler und das stolze Fräulein," the Florentine setting leads Rilke to a condemnation of crowded composition, which he sees as a corollary of the Renaissance desire to crowd as much as possible into one's lifetime. His ironic condemnation of this dense composition recalls to us that Michelangelo deplored this tendency: ". . . so fehlt daran in Wahrheit doch die rechte Kunst, das rechte Mass, und das rechte Verhältnis, sowie Auswahl und klare Verteilung im Raume und schliesslich selbst Nerv und Substanz."[56] In this tale there is a direct reference to Michelangelo; the heroine is described as being "stolz wie ein Stein in den Händen Michelangelos,"[57] a factitious conceit not particularly Buonarrotian. In "Ein Verein aus einem dringenden Bedürfnis heraus" the theme is the foundation of an artist's colony, which has prompted Rilke scholars to a gratuitous and unlikely comparison with Worpswede. Three touches of Michelangelo's aesthetics reappear herein more or less identifiable as such. The artist's known disinclination to talk about art, attested by De Hollanda, Giannotti, and others, is reflected in "Die drei Maler sprachen natürlich nicht von Kunst."[58] Michelangelo's belief in an artistic elect endowed at birth with an *intelletto* ("Nel parto mi fu data la bellezza")[59] seems implicit in the characterization: "es wirkliche Künstler waren, gewissermassen von der Natur beabsichtigte. . . ."[60] The working together of the eye and hand, a simple enough arrangement which had become a "principle"

56. De Hollanda, *Vier Gespräche,* p. 29.
57. *Geschichten,* p. 155.
58. *Ibid.,* p. 137.
59. Frey, *Dichtungen,* p. 99.
60. Rilke, *Geschichten,* p. 137.

in Plotinus, was restated as a principle by Michelangelo on several occasions,[61] and especially in his often quoted statement, "che bisognava avere le seste negli occhi e non in mano, perchè le mani operano e l'occhio giudica."[62] It is recalled when members of Rilke's art colony see style as the product of "den Blick, die Hand und wie alle die Dinge heissen, ohne welche ein Maler zwar leben, aber nicht malen kann."[63] In the final tale, "Eine Geschichte dem Dunkel erzählt," there seems no possible pretext to evoke Buonarroti; the tone of other stories has been abandoned; yet, when the narrator Georg asks his old friend Klara the name and profession of the man she married, she replies, "Angelo ist Maler."[64]

It is uncritical and unhistorical to assert that the ascendancy of Rodin is felt in these stories, to conjecture, as an excellent student of Rilke has done recently, that "the divine sculptor of the stories may have been modelled on Rodin."[65] Rilke composed these stories almost three years before he met Rodin for the first time, and the strong influence was to occur later. Rodin's marble *Main de Dieu* dates from 1902, two years after the publication of the *Geschichten*. None of Rilke's letters or journals— nor the monograph on Rodin—would indicate an influence by Rodin as early as 1899, any more than do the *Geschichten* themselves, even though Rilke had been introduced to the work of Rodin through Lepsius in 1897. In 1899, Michelangelo, as thinker and poet much more than practitioner, exercised an ascendancy over Rainer Rilke and the intellectually alert of his generation. The poetic and philosophic side of the Florentine master was newly revealed in those documentary sources to which we have been referring the reader throughout this essay. Our inquiry would indicate that even at this moment Rilke had started to familiarize himself with and form preferences among those sonnets, madrigals, and *canzoni* on which he worked most intensely after 1914. If he failed to publish, for one reason or another, poems commonly used since his time to explain Michelangelo's aesthetics ("Per fido esemplo alla mia uocazione" and

---

61. See R. J. Clements, "Mind, Eye, and Hand in Michelangelo's Poetry," *PMLA*, LXIX (1954), 324-36.

62. Vasari, *Le Vite*, VII, 270.

63. *Geschichten*, p. 140.   64. *Ibid.*, p. 172.

65. E. M. Butler, *Rainer Maria Rilke* (Cambridge, 1941), p. 101. This work, however, briefly supposes a strong and increasing Buonarrotian influence on Rilke, and suggests that this influence incited the heaven-storming page in his 1898 diary.

"Non ha l'ottimo artista alcun concetto"), his absorption with the
ethos and psyche of that artist made him translate Michelangelo's
most intimate mystical revelations ("Giunta gia è 'l corso della
uita mia," "Per qual mordace lima," "Non fur men lieti che tur-
bati e tristi," etc.). One cannot draw facile conclusions, however,
from the absence of certain poems from his translations, since Rilke
abandoned various pieces because of their difficulty or obscurity (he
apparently did not utilize the Guasti edition with its paraphrases
in a simpler Italian).

To an extent, then, the *Geschichten* afford more direct perceptions of Rilke's interest in Michelangelo than do the *Dichtungen*. Rilke's translations from the *Rime* are so faithful
("genaue und reine," in his words) that there is no room for
himself in them. (They are, incidentally, better and more literal
than the English equivalents of Symonds, done two decades
earlier, although both unfortunately attempted to retain rhyme.)
Rilke admitted this to Ellen Delp. "Nein, natürlich spreche
ich nicht Meiniges in ihnen aus, wenn ich sie meiner Sprache
zu fassen gebe ... nicht von meinen Verhängnissen handeln sie."[66]
But Rilke the storyteller interwove elements from the *Rime*,
the *Lettere*, and the biographies reflecting not only Michelangelo's
aesthetic *Anschauung* but also those moments when the Florentine
was "in tanta passione." Rilke, as he wrote more than once, was
shortly thereafter to find strength and joy and purpose in Rodin,
who faced his personal and professional problems with stoicism
and resignation. Yet his discovery of Michelangelo, who like himself poured all his *Seelenangst* into his letters and poems and
who faced as a young and dedicated artist some of the same problems which were already beginning to torment Rilke as the
century closed, could not fail to afford the comfort and encourage-
ment of *sympatheia*.

It has been supposed that Rilke's association with Rodin, who
had written that the Florentine had "held out his powerful hand
to me" and saved him from the academism of Ingres,[67] heightened
Rilke's interest in Michelangelo. It has also been supposed that
the admitted influence of Rodin in making Rilke view art as
an artist rather than as a *littérateur* gave the younger man a new
approach to Michelangelo. The *Geschichten vom lieben Gott* of
1899 disprove the first supposition and the *Dichtungen des Michelangelo* of 1914-23 invalidate the second.

66. Rilke, *Briefe* (Wiesbaden, 1950), II, 292.
67. Judith Cladel, *Rodin* (New York, 1937), p. 46.

III

DESPORTES AND PETRARCH

PHILIPPE DESPORTES, France's most popular poet at the close of the French Renaissance, has been universally accepted as a Petrarchist. Availing himself of the current license, not to say obligation, to plagiarize from earlier writers under the guise of imitation or "innutrition," he borrowed unstintingly from the Italian Petrarchists of the Quattrocento and early Cinquecento: Chariteo, Tebaldeo, Serafino, Sasso, and Ariosto. Judging from the plagiarisms already brought to light, one would conclude that Desportes took more from certain of these Petrarchists than from Petrarch himself. When Lavaud, in his careful study on Desportes, lists the Italian sources of the poems in *Diane I*, *Diane II*, *Hippolyte*, and *Cléonice*, his tabulation shows that Desportes "imitated" Petrarch nine times, while cribbing from Antonio Tebaldeo thirteen times and from Pamfilo Sasso ten times.[1]

The purpose of this essay is to adjust the record by bringing to light twelve undetected plagiarisms from Petrarch in Desportes's poetry. It will attempt to give the devil his due, re-establishing Desportes as a more unadulterated Petrarchist through the rather curious *rapprochement* of literary larceny.

If the borrowings of Desportes vary from sheer translation to very loose, almost imperceptible, imitation, let us remember that the Renaissance doctrine of mimesis sanctioned both extreme types of appropriation. In the terminology of his countryman, Joachim du Bellay, Desportes ran the gamut of *traducteur* (translates verbatim), *translateur* (reproduces ideas closely), *paraphraste* (reproduces ideas freely), and *imitateur* (practices innutrition). Usually, although not always, Desportes's borrowings place him in one of the latter two categories.

As early as 1579, twenty-seven years before the death of Desportes, Henri Estienne showed that Desportes' "Aspre et sauvage cœur, trop fière volonté" had its origin in Petrarch's "Aspro cor e selvaggio, e cruda voglia."[2] In 1583 a Gascon poet, Augié Gaillard, accused Desportes of drawing upon Petrarch, but without citing specific examples.[3] In recent times the scholars who

---

1. Jacques Lavaud, *Philippe Desportes* (Paris, 1935), pp. 175, 179, 180, 283.
2. H. Estienne, *De la précellence du langage françois* (Paris, n.d.), p. 238.
3. J. Lavaud, *op. cit.*, p. 176.

have listed most carefully the Italian sources of Desportes are
Francesco Flamini, J. Vianey, and J. Lavaud.[4] To present the
reader with the complete background, we shall include in a footnote the nine plagiarisms from Petrarch which have been brought
to light over the past three and a half centuries,[5] with the necessary advice, "Non ragioniam di loro, ma guarda e passa." We
now pass to the enumeration of twelve heretofore unidentified
plagiarisms, while the voice of Malherbe must be applauding
somewhere in the Stygian darkness.

Frequently Desportes followed Petrarch's incipit fairly closely
and then wandered off to his own devices, keeping within the
general framework of Petrarch's argument and only occasionally
revealing his source by a similarity of expression. Thus, Des-

4. F. Flamini, *Studi di storia letteraria* (Livorno, 1895), pp. 433-39; J.
Vianey, *Le pétrarquisme en France au XVIe siècle* (Montpellier, 1909), pp.
222-56. Also, Vianey's "Une rencontre des Muses" in *Revue d'histoire littéraire,*
XIII (1906), 92-100.

5. We shall list only the incipits; a table of incipits may be found in Lavaud
and in most editions of Petrarch's *Rime:*

> Desp.: "Si foy plus certaine en une âme non feinte"
> Pet.: "S' una fede amorosa, un cor non finto"
> Desp.: "Ma nef passe au destroit d'une mer courroucée"
> Pet.: "Passa la nave mia colma d'obblio"
> Desp.: "Amour en mesme instant m'aiguillonne et m'arreste"
> Pet.: "Amor mi sprona in un tempo ed affrena"
> Desp.: "A pas lens et tardifs tout seul je me promaine"
> Pet.: "Solo e pensoso i più deserti campi"
> Desp.: "Solitaire et pensif, dans un bois écarté"
> Pet.: "Solo e pensoso i più deserti campi"
> Desp.: "Aspre et sauvage cœur, trop fière volonté"
> Pet.: "Aspro cor e selvaggio e cruda voglia"

Of the three remaining plagiarisms, the first is mentioned by Vianey, *op cit.,*
p. 251 ("Chargé du desespoir qui trouble ma pensée"). This claim is accepted
by Lavaud, who adds the remaining two *rencontres,* pp. 179, 283 ("Blessé d'une
playe inhumaine"; "Les celestes beautez d'une heureuse jeunesse"). However, in no case is the purported Petrarchan source specifically explained. Nor
is it mentioned in any of the source studies (Flamini, Vianey, Vaganay, Kastner, Cameron) to which Lavaud refers his reader (p. 178). Lavaud does not
mention the charge of plagiarism made in Vaganay's edition of *Les amours
d'Hippolyte,* p. 16 ("Je vay contant les jours et les heures passées"), which
charge also lacks documentation. Nor does he mention two alleged plagiarisms
advanced by Vianey, pp. 303, 304 ("Quand, miroir de moy-mesme, en moy
je me regarde"/"Quand' io mi volgo indietro a mirar gli anni"; "Le jour
chasse le jour, comme un flot l'autre chasse"/*Trionfo della morte,* I, 82). The
first of these claims seems questionable and the second untenable. the themes
involved are commonplace and the wordings dissimilar.

portes derived an "elegy" in the *Amours d'Hippolyte* from sonnet CLII of Petrarch.[6] Decrying the cruelty of his mistress,

> Ayez le cœur d'un tigre ou d'une ourse cruelle[7]

> Questa umil fera, un cor di tigre o d'orsa[8]

he states that love wounds and poisons him (envenimez ma playe / dolce veneno). While Desportes rambles on for fifty-six verses, he finally returns to the thought that after so many trials (tant de cruautez / tante varietati), there is no way out other than death, a decision identical with Petrarch's:

> Mais, quand vous me jurez, je chante vos beautez . . .
> Car je me suis promis que vous me seriez telle,
> Et n'atten pas de vous un plus doux traitement,
> Que mourir sans pitié

> Fuggendo [morendo] spera i suoi dolor finire;
> Come colei che d'ora in ora manca:
> Chè ben puo nulla chi non puo morire.

The simple theme of the lover's dread of the approaching lonely night would seem to be sufficiently universal to occur to an amorous poet without the intermediary of a literary source. However, Desportes feeds parasitically upon Petrarch's emotions when he copies even this theme. We cite only those lines showing the closest resemblance:

> Tout le jour mes deux yeux sont de pleurs dégoutans,
> Puis quand la nuit paisible en repos nous rappelle,
> Ma douleur s'envenime et devient si rebelle,
> Que du tout je me lasche aux regrets esclatans.
> En si piteux estat je despense mon tans,
> Me paissant dans mon cœur[9]

> Tutt' il dì piango; e poi, la notte, quando
> Prendon riposo i miseri mortali,
> Trovom' in pianto e raddoppiarsi i mali:
> Cosi spendo 'l mio tempo lagrimando.
> In tristo umor vo gli occhi consumando,
> E 'l cor in doglia;[10]

---

6. Our page references hereafter will apply to the Michiels edition of Desportes (Paris, 1858) and the Scherillo edition of Petrarch's *Rime* (Milan, 1925), which enjoyed a wide circulation.

7. Desportes, Michiels edition (Paris, 1858), p. 138.

8. Petrarch, *Rime*, Scherillo edition (Milan, 1925), p. 318. Petrarch's last verse echoes Seneca, *Decl.* II: "Quicquam non potest, qui mori non potest."

9. Desportes, *op. cit.*, p. 486.

10. Petrarch, *op. cit.*, p. 381.

Each sonnet continues decrying the poet's mental state and each likens life to a living death.

Desportes derived a longer piece, a *plainte* addressed to Diane, from this same Petrarchan sonnet. The theme may be summed up in six verses:

> Depuis l'aube du jour, je n'ay point eu de cesse
> De pleurer, de crier et de me tourmenter . . .
> Le jour s'est retiré, voicy la nuit veneuë,
> Qui soulage les cœurs des hommes travaillez;
> Mais, plus fière tousjours, ma douleur continuë,
> Et vainqueurs du sommeil, mes maux sont éveillez.[11]

If Desportes borrowed the theme, he borrowed nothing else. Once the French poet develops it wordily, it ceases to be Petrarchan in spirit.

One of the more unusual plagiarisms occurs among Desportes's epitaphs. Penning a sonnet on the death of his mistress, he betrays no Petrarchan source until he reaches the sestet. Only upon reading the sestet do we suddenly discern that the sentiment of the epitaph is second-hand and synthetic:

> L'air, la terre et les eaux cet outrage ont pleuré,
> Le monde, en la perdant, sans lustre est demeuré,
> Comme un pré sans couleurs, un bois sans robe verte,
>   Tandis qu'il en jouit, il ne la connut pas;
> Moy seul je la connus, qui la pleure icy-bas,
> Cependant que le ciel s'enrichit de ma perte.[12]

> Pianger l'aer e la terra e 'l mar devrebbe
> L'uman legnaggio, che senz' ella è quasi
> Senza fior prato, o senza gemma anello.
>   Non la conobbe il mondo mentre l'ebbe:
> Conobbil' io, ch' a pianger qui rimasi,
> E'l Ciel, che del mio pianto or si fa bello.[13]

When Peletier, Sébilet, Ronsard, and Du Bellay were encouraging their contemporaries to "imitate" in this manner, they should at least have drawn the line on epitaphs.

Petrarch's sonnet berating his tongue for freezing into timid silence in Laura's presence caught the fancy of Desportes, who copied its sonnet form and retained its spirit:

11. Desportes, *op. cit., p.* 42.
12. Desportes, *op. cit.,* p. 486.
13. Petrarch, *Rime,* Scherillo edition (Milan, 1925), pp. 524–25. We first mentioned this plagiarism in a discussion of *imitatio* in sixteenth-century France: *Critical Theory and Practice of the Pléiade* (Cambridge, 1942), pp. 262–63.

Langue muette, à mon secours tardive,
Que m'a servi tant d'heur que j'ay reçeu
De voir ma dame? aussi bien tu n'as sçeu
Dire le mal qui de repos me prive? . . .
Car un seul mot hors de moy n'est issu
Propre à monstrer combien ma peine est vive.[14]

Perch'io t'abbia guardato di menzogna
A mio podere, ed onorato assai,
Ingrata lingua, già pero non m'hai
Renduto onor, ma fatto ira e vergogna;
    Che quando più 'l tuo aiuto mi bisogna
Per dimandar mercede, allor ti stai
Sempre più fredda; e se parole fai,
sono imperfette, e quasi d'uom che sogna.[15]

Both poets then proceed to blame their other senses for failing them in like manner.

Desportes apparently borrowed from Petrarch his theme of the inimical hand. He introduced it both in Book II of *Diane* ("Belle et cruelle main, qui m'avez enchaisné") and in the *Diverses amours*, XVIII. In the latter piece, Desportes, like Petrarch, laments his mistress' hand which grips his heart:

Je la doy bien hayr, cette main ennemye,
Qui décocha sur moy tant de traits rigoureux,
Et du sang de ma playe, encor tout chaloureux,
M'escrivit dans le cœur le nom de Parthenie.[16]

O bella man che mi distringi il core
E 'n poco spazio la mia vita chiudi;
Man ov' ogni arte e tutti loro studi
Poser Natura e 'l Ciel per farsi onore.[17]

To close this would-be *blason* to milady's hand, each of the poets praises her glove in gallant fashion:

Au moins baisons son gand. Il est tousjours permis
De baiser le dessus d'un sacré reliquaire.

Candido, leggiadretto e caro guanto,
Che copria netto avorio e fresche rose.

One piece in the *Diverses amours* (XXXIII) sums up in a few lines a typical Petrarchan sonnet ("L'aura celeste che 'n

14. Desportes, Michiels edition (Paris, 1858), p. 167.
15. Petrarch, *op cit.*, p. 174. This seems a more probable source than Chariteo's "Quando, da presso, il bel guardo sereno."
16. Desportes, *op. cit.*, p. 388.
17. Petrarch, *op. cit.*, p. 359.

quel verde lauro") and devotes the remaining lines to a tergi-versation, explaining how Desportes's feelings altered from those described by Petrarch. He explains how he has borne the yoke of love,

> Quand je portoy le joug de vostre tyrannie[18]

> Ed a me pose un dolce giogo al collo,[19]

how the mere shadow of his mistress intimidated him,

> Je vous craignoy si fort, que l'ombre seulement
> D'un seul de vos dédains m'estoit peine infinie;

> L'ombra sua sola fa 'l mio cor un ghiaccio,

and how the infidelities of his mistress have finally cured him of such fears. This borrowing is extraordinary, for Desportes here compresses rather than amplifies the Petrarchan text.

Petrarch's image of Laura as his resplendent Sun, traditional though it was, evidently pleased Desportes. He cribbed in a more or less elastic manner from two Petrarchan sonnets containing the image. In the first instance, milady is compared to the morning sun. Desportes, like Petrarch, begins his sonnet with Phoebus driving his golden chariot over the horizon before the oncoming stars:

> Quand l'ombrageuse nuit nostre jour décolore,
> Et que le clair Phœbus se cache en l'Occident,
> Au ciel d'astres semé les mortels regardant. . . .[20]

> Quando 'l Sol bagna in mar l'aurato carro,
> E l'aer nostro e la mia mente imbruna,
> Col cielo e con le stelle e con la luna. . . .[21]

But the night is dispelled in turn by a welcome morning sun returning to outshine the stars. Desportes's Hippolyta (Marguerite de Valois?), more lustrous and radiant than other women, is like the early sun blotting out the stars. In Petrarch, Laura is paragoned to a sun which brings warmth and delight after a troubled night.

In the second instance, milady becomes the vernal sun,

19. Petrarch, *op cit.*, p. 357.

18. Desportes, *op. cit.*, p. 401.

20. Desportes, *op. cit.*, p. 166. A discreet adaptation of this image was made by Desportes in his memorial sonnet to Diane de Cossé, Countess of Mansfeld ("Quand le soleil nous laisse et que, tout radieux"), where he laments the gloom and darkness left on earth by the setting of this sun "gone to the other hemisphere" (p. 468).

21. Petrarch, *op. cit.*, p. 387.

bringing the heat and color of April. The warm feeling of spring-
time which his sun should create is, however, denied each poet.
In Petrarch it is because Laura turns her rays from him; in
Desportes, because Hippolyta hides them from him. If its treatment differs in the two poets, the theme itself remains the same.
Thus, we may conclude that Desportes's "Quand le soleil doré
laisse nostre hemisphère" (page 139) is an echo, with added over-
and undertones, of Petrarch's "Quando 'l pianeta che distingue
l'ore."

Desportes, like Petrarch, centers a poem upon the thought
that a lover once freed from the bonds of love avoids entangle-
ment another time. In each case it is the death of his mistress
which has freed the poet:

> Avec un si beau nœud l'Amour m'avoit contraint,
> Qu'encor qu'il soit rompu j'en sens tousjours l'estrainte . . .
> Que la mort donc se vante, ayant frappé ma dame.[22]

> L'ardente nodo ov' io fui d'ora in ora.
> Contando anni ventuno interi, preso,
> Morte disciolse.[23]

Petrarch toys with the idea in greater detail, specifying that Love
tempted him yet again, but that once more Death saved him
from becoming involved.

Petrarch's sonnet describing the devastation which Laura's
eyes worked upon him impressed Desportes sufficiently for the
latter to imitate it loosely. The *capoversi* reveal the inspiration:

> Si doucement par son regard me tue[24]

> Se 'l dolce sguardo di costei m'ancide[25]

Each piece then explains how the mistress' eyes affect the poet's
moods through their strange power. Each poet trembles before
them (Je tremble tout / s' i' tremo). While the eyes of Desportes's
Hippolyta assemble all contrary moods and impart them to him,
Petrarch similarly notes the contrary moods of his lady with the
Vergilian reminiscence, "Femmina è cosa mobil per natura."

We arrive now at the final plagiarism on our list. Sonnet
LVI of *Diane II* ("Tant d'amour, tant de foy, dont vos lettres
sont plaines") evidently derives from sonnet CLXVIII of Petrarch ("Amor mi manda quel dolce pensiero"). Diana has sent

22. Desportes, Michiels edition (Paris, 1858), p. 486.
23. Petrarch, *Rime*, Scherillo edition (Milan, 1925), p. 448.
24. Desportes, *op. cit.*, p. 158.
25. Petrarch, *op. cit.*, p. 344.

Desportes a billet doux encouraging his passion, but he suspects insincerity; he begs for some proof of her affection more tangible than empty words. Petrarch writes that Love has sent him a message to the effect that Laura loves him and is ready to accede to him; however, having had occasion to find Love's words untrue, he remains much in doubt. Both poets introduce the *carpe florem* theme: time is fleeting and the season for love is at hand. Diana and Laura are getting older as well as their lovers:

> Depuis quatre ans entiers vous m'appastez ainsi;
> Je vieillis cependant, vous vieillissez aussi
> Et perdons de nos ans la saison mieux aimée.[26]

> In questa passa 'l tempo, e nello specchio
> Mi veggio andar ver la stagion contraria
> A sua impromessa et alla mia speranza.
> Or sia che puo: già sol io non invecchio.[27]

While the *carpe diem* of Horace or the *carpe florem* of Ausonius was a common theme among Ronsard, Baïf, Du Bellay, and their contemporaries, it seems apparent here that it is again from Petrarch that Desportes has plagiarized.

Having proposed a dozen examples of Petrarchan influence concerning which there can be little doubt, we daunt superstition to add a possible thirteenth. Desportes's sonnet "Si les pleurs que j'espans, si le triste langage" (page 156) borrows a theme without any textual translation. It has its apparent source in Petrarch's "Amor, Fortuna, e la mia mente schiva."[28] The text of each piece is that Love and Fortune engage in a war of attrition against the poets, inducing the latter to contemplate suicide.

To complete the picture we must mention briefly a few of the many borrowings of isolated verses and images which are not developed to an appreciable extent. Typical is the following set of conceits:

> Ma Dame, Amour, Fortune, et tous les elemens
> Animez contre moy, sont bandez pour ne nuire.[29]

> Amor, Natura, e la bell' alma umile,
> Ov' ogni alta virtude alberga e regna,
> Contra me son giurati.[30]

26. Desportes, *op. cit.*, p. 104.
27. Petrarch, *op. cit.*, p. 332.
28. Petrarch, *op. cit.*, p. 267.
29. Desportes, *op. cit.*, p. 71.
30. Petrarch, *op. cit.*, p. 345.

Or, again:

> Malheureux fut le jour, le mois et la saison
> Que le cruel Amour ensorcela mon ame.[31]

> Benedetto sia 'l giorno e 'l mese e l'anno
> E la stagione e 'l tempo e l'ora e 'l punto
> E 'l bel paese e 'l loco ov' io fui giunto
> Da duo begli occhi, che legato m'hanno.[32]

Other *rencontres* worthy of mention are the metaphor of the lover and the salamander living in flame,[33] the promise to love so long as the stars shine in the sky,[34] the complaint about love's harsh law (sauvage loy d'amour / dura legge d'amor),[35] and the famous simile which was so widely appropriated by the poets of the Pléiade:

> Le lit en mes pensers est un champ de bataille.[36]

> E duro campo di battaglia il letto.[37]

The reader will probably grant that no Renaissance poet's works illustrate better than Desportes's the range from slavish translation to the more creative innutrition (free reworking of the earlier model). Both types of imitation were held in high esteem during the sixteenth century.[38] Even in his "innutritions" Desportes usually translates the incipit of his source quite closely before wandering off to his own thoughts and imagery. He seems thus to prefer stressing his dependent rather than his independent thinking. He is fully aware that a translation of the incipit is the surest way to reveal his plagiarizing. But as a *translateur* or *paraphraste* in the Renaissant (and Du Bellayan) sense, he has utterly no reason to disguise his cribbing.

Having resorted to mathematics in our first paragraph, we return to that science. To the nine plagiarisms previously detected we now add our dozen. Thus, whereas the record originally admitted a greater number of borrowings from such Petrarchists

31. Desportes, *op. cit.*, p. 32.
32. Petrarch, *Rime*, Scherillo edition (Milan, 1925), p. 191. Evidently Petrarch himself derived this conceit in turn from the Provençal poets, possibly from Giraut de Borneill: "Ben aia 'l temps e 'l jorns e l'ans e 'l mes, . . ."
33. Desportes, Michiels edition (Paris, 1858), p. 27; Petrarch, *op. cit.*, p. 369.
34. Desportes, Michiels edition (Paris, 1858), p. 27; Petrarch, *op. cit.*, p. 355.
35. Desportes, *op. cit.*, p. 125; Petrarch, *T.A.* 148.
36. Desportes, *op. cit.*, p. 17.
37. Petrarch, *Rime*, Scherillo edition (Milan, 1925), p. 389.
38. Richard McKeon, "Concept of Imitation," *Modern Philology*, XXXIV (1936), 1-37.

as Tebaldeo and Sasso, Petrarch himself now heads the list, being the source of twenty-one plagiarisms, or as the French more delicately put it, *rapprochements*. Desportes's Petrarchism becomes more nearly a direct imitation of the archetype than of other Petrarchists. We no longer need condemn Desportes as an imitator of imitations, much as Plato condemned the μιμητικὸς ποιητής for imitating the imitated forms of nature (*Republic*, x).

True, Desportes was such a prolific Petrarchist that even these relatively few borrowings out of his total production of sonnets may not seem to detract much from his originality. But there were other Petrarchistic models he copied: Amalteo, Amanio, Caro, Mozzarello, Molza, Tansillo. And in addition to these instances where Desportes borrowed the letter, there were others, many others, where he borrowed the spirit. The "innutrition" became so complete that the source can be sensed where it cannot be perceived. By imitating, by strapping onto his Pegasus the saddlebags of Petrarchistic conceits and themes, he weakened his poetry and, like so many of his contemporaries, contributed to the ill repute in which Petrarchism was held during the last decades of the sixteenth century. Leaning on his models, in text or spirit, Desportes could not hope to better them. Only rarely, when creating independently (*e.g.*, his *chansons*), does Desportes come near rivaling them. Yet we must not be severe with Desportes' shortcomings. They resulted naturally from the great weakness of the Renaissance conception of *imitatio*, the product of a chronological inferiority complex and the misunderstanding of a term of classical rhetoric. The key word of Renaissance literary theory should have been *æmulatio*, not *imitatio*. The whole difficulty lies right there.

Included in the *Diverses amours* is a sonnet entitled "Pour mettre devant un Pétrarque" which begins:

> Le labeur glorieux d'un esprit admirable
> Triomphe heureusement de la postérité,
> Comme ce Florentin qui a si bien chanté
> Que les siècles d'après n'ont trouvé son semblable.[39]

Adducing as evidence the plagiarisms of the letter and of the spirit noted throughout this article, one may give the lie to the last line and charge Desportes himself with being the *semblable*.

39. Desportes, *op. cit.*, p. 427.

IV

LITERARY THEORY AND CRITICISM IN SCALIGER'S
POEMATA

WITHIN a few short years after his death at Agen in 1558, Julius-Caesar Scaliger had become recognized as the most serious literary theorist of his day, in direct succession from Aristotle through Horace and Vida. Some bedazzled contemporaries even ruled Vida out of this company, leaving Scaliger nonpareil in the Renaissance.[1] His slightly posthumous *Poetices libri septem* (1561) was a formidable summa of more stylistic and rhetorical devices, more forms, genres, classifications and subclassifications than anyone ever assembled before or since, to say nothing of their wealth of speculation and theory common to other Renaissance *artes poeticae*.[2] The Latin of this classic in the history of literary theory is at times "tourmenté" (Lintilhac) and "perplexing" (Padelford), as alleged, but its most characteristic quality is lifelessness. It is the inert Latin which one would find in a contemporary herbal or a treatise on gynecology, which are coincidentally the subjects of two of Scaliger's other books. Had he composed all his works in French, he would have remained for posterity one of the half-dozen most quoted authors of sixteenth-century France. But then, to paraphrase his epigram on Dolet, he would not be Scaliger. In any case, his very influential *Poetices* presents the picture of a cold analyst defining and classifying and, in the sections *Criticus* and *Hypercriticus*, venturing sober criticisms of safely established authors of the past "provided that they are dead and published." Curiously, this important tractate has never been translated into any vernacular, never reappeared in a modern, accessible reprint, and has been the object of relatively little investigation.[3]

1. López Pinciano, for example, finds the poetics of Scaliger a better tool than the treatises of either Horace or Vida: *Philosophía antigua poética* (Madrid, 1953), I, 9-10.

2. Julius Caesar Scaliger, *Poetices libri septem* (Lyon, 1561). My personal copy, to which footnotes are keyed, is the Geneva edition of 1581.

3. The major books have been: Eugène Lintilhac, *De Julii Caesaris Scaligeri poetice* (Paris, 1890); Eduard Brinkschulte, *Julius Caesar Scaligers kunsttheoretische Anschauungen* (Bonn, 1913); F. M. Padelford, *Selected Translations from Scaliger's Poetics* (New York, 1905); Vernon Hall, *Life of Julius Caesar Scaliger* (Philadelphia, 1950). Hall's extensive bibliography and his sections on Scaliger's relations with his contemporaries have been invaluable in the preparation of this study.

Yet there was another Julius-Caesar Scaliger even less known and studied. That was Scaliger the poet, who revealed himself as a more personal and subjective writer in the corpus of Latin poetry published by his learned and loyal son Joseph in 1574.[4] A few section titles of the two parts show the variety of tone and topic of the works included: *apiculae, satyrae, epigrammata, anacreontica, lacrymae, logogriphi, hymni, etc.* Scaliger the poet, however, is never free of Scaliger the theorist and critic. It is well known that in Renaissance France poets theorized and theorists poetized. As I have written elsewhere, the creative writers theorized and criticized in their works of every genre, with the exception of their orisons. "Ronsard spares only his God from shop talk about literary acquaintances."[5] In the *Poemata* Scaliger returns again and again to specific theories, clothing them in original imagery and personal interpretation. He devotes poems to individual writers from antiquity down to his own day, vivid and lively passages in which he more than once loses that objectivity so carefully preserved in the *Poetices libri.* Only one scholar has remarked in passing on the tremendous value of the opinions and comments in the *Poemata.* De Santi wrote back in 1905, "Je fus frappé de la richesse et de la variété des renseignements que cet indigeste pandémonium peut fournir à l'histoire littéraire du XVIe siècle,"[6] but no one has exploited the vein thus pointed out. Indeed, these theories and criticisms should be examined as complementing, supplementing, or refuting ideas in the *Poetices libri* or Scaliger's other works on oratory, language, and literature.[7] After the orderly listing and classifying in the *Poetices libri,* the "coq-à-l'asne" character of the *Poemata* comes as a relief.

Reading the *Poemata,* one does not need the violent tracts against Erasmus and Cardan[8] to understand why Scaliger was known as "le tondeur." Compared with some of his judgments

---

4. Julius Caesar Scaliger, *Poemata in duas partes diuisa* (Heidelberg, 1574). My copy, to which footnotes refer, is the Geneva edition of 1591.

5. R. J. Clements, *Critical Theory and Practice of the Pléiade* (Cambridge, 1942), p. xii.

6. L. De Santi, "Rabelais et J. C. Scaliger," *Revue des études rabelaisiennes,* III (1905), 12-44.

7. Such as his *De causis linguae latinae* of 1540, his *De comoediae origine* of 1568, and his *Orationes pro Cicerone* of 1531 and 1535.

8. The *Orationes* mentioned in the previous note were directed against Erasmus; against Cardan he wrote his *Exotericarum exercitationum liber XV in Cardanum de subtilitate* of 1555.

in the *Poemata* on Rabelais, Dolet, and Cardan, Malherbe's marginalia on Desportes were like the soft-spoken chidings of a doting uncle. Erasmus psychoanalyzed Scaliger as one who sought antagonists. In general, Scaliger's literary attacks cannot be dismissed as mere exercises in the tradition of Archilochus, even though one of the sections of the *Poemata* is entitled after that irascible ancient. Robert Burton could not fail to see the irony in Scaliger's assurance to Cardan, "Didst know me well, thou wouldst not only pardon these my witticisms, but would even consider it unmeet that so kindly a soul as I should find it necessary to avert even the slightest suspicion."[9] There are, of course, kindly and even gracious criticisms in the *Poemata*. Thus it becomes important not only to determine the criteria adopted in these comments on ancient and Renaissance writers, but also to try to understand the motivations behind them.

The literary observations in the *Poemata* worthy of recording will be classified into three groups:

I. General literary theories or motifs
II. Comments on ancient writers
III. Comments on Renaissance writers

The first poem of the collection, after the dedication to Brassac, explains "Quare versus faciat" ("Si mea mens ulla potuit ratione moveri").[10] It expresses the theory of artistic compulsion which reappeared about this time in Michelangelo's admission, "Io non posso vivere non che dipigniere."[11] Scaliger is not sure whether it is fate ("numen") or chance which drives him on, to versifying in his lonely room, to living in fear of critics and adverse fame when he could be leading a relaxed life of social dinners and appearances at court. This quest of the poet for honor is as foolish as the soldier's illusions about dying for glory. For all the strength he derives from Apollo and Aristotle he may never attain fickle fame. Yet it is all the same to him. He will live and write in his ivory tower. Besides articulating the theory of poetic compulsion and justifying the ivory tower, this piece implies a criticism of the court poets of the type of Mellin de

9. Robert Burton, *The Anatomy of Melancholy* (New York, 1938), pp. 103-4. See Appendix.

10. *Poemata*, 1, 2. All future references to *Poemata* will be given in parentheses in main text of this essay.

11. G. Milanesi, *Le Lettere di Michelangelo Buonarroti* (Florence, 1875), p. 488.

Saint-Gelays and perhaps even Ronsard, though Scaliger will toss them small bouquets later on.

This poem, with its mentions of Apollo and the Muses, might lead one to conclude that Scaliger subscribed to the belief in natural inspiration. One of his pieces, "Musarum otium," pays lip service to the notion of spontaneous inspiration. Scaliger has felt, says the poem, that much of his production is laughable, weak, wanting in elegance, and trampled by foolishness. He has reached the point of giving up poetry. But fires of great strength often crawl along the ground. Just when he is ready to give up, nature comes to his rescue:

> atque ibi tentat
> Porro ex informi terentem procudere versum.   (*Poemata*, I, 42.)

Slowly he becomes warmed up and excited and the words begin to issue forth. This description of the visitation of the poetic fury should be matched against its dramatization in Ronsard's *La lyre*.

It stands to reason that the theory of nature as the exclusive formative agent behind poetry could hardly have been more than a poetic motif for this rational critic and grammarian whose *Poetices libri* are a monument to the premise that one cannot become a poet without the diligent study of *character, perspicuitas, proprietas, numerositas, sonus*, and a multitude of other properties of poetry and rhetoric. Indeed, the fourth book of his poetic art bears the meaningful title of "parasceve." It was a common paradox that all the writers of Renaissance *artes poeticae*, after devoting their first chapters or "books" to the doctrine of natural genius and the imagery of inspiration, devoted their remaining pages to instruction in the techniques to be mastered by the beginner. The same, by the way, was true of the *artes pictoriae* of the period.

Thus Scaliger recedes to the Horatian and Quintilian compromise taken by most of his contemporaries. An excellent statement of this position accepting art and nature as "conjurateurs à la perfection du poète" (Sébilet) is found in his "epidorpidian" poem, "Ingenium paratur agro." Here he draws an analogy with a field of wild thorn bushes and biting brambles which produces a better and greater yield after it has been "pacified" by the plowshare and seeded with care. (II, 187.) This medial position is again revealed in the three-lined "Ingenium excultum":

Vsu nitidus, cote vel artis expolitus
Vir, vel Genio compositus sibi sermo:
Vir nae ille virorum est merus, aut deus pusillus. (II, 160.)

Scaliger betrays throughout his works, however, the Renaissance conviction that the most ancient poets (θεόπνευστοι in his words) were the spontaneous creations of that nature and divinity to which they lived in such close proximity.

Another Horatian compromise accepted by Scaliger concerns the useful and the sweet purposes of poetry. From his *Poetices libri* we learn his feeling that epic should polish and reform mores and that poetry should "docere cum iucunditate."[12] This polishing and therapeutic function is confirmed in "Poesi expolitur animus":

Anni vitia, atque aeris inuidum uenenum
Urgente precum carmine decedere credunt.
Tun' tergi animos carmine, & ambiges poliri? (II, 190.)

The power of "Poetae utiles," as another piece is called, lies in the principle of katharsis or empathy which makes their readers or listeners believe themselves present at the "miserable flames" of Troy. This power of holding is like "sirenum blanditiae," a Boethian image reappearing in Sidney as "syrens sweetness." The poets also teach virtue, Scaliger recalls, by extolling holy or exemplary men (II, 125); he himself attempts this in his sections "Heroes" and "Heroinae."

The Pindaric cult of glory and artistic self-awareness, so prominent among the Pléiade group, is very real to Scaliger. In "Commendat opus suum aeternitati," he petitions blessed fame to preserve his works "usque ad orbis ultimos dies." (I, 349.) The poet is a noble being "whose breast is uninhabitable to imperfection," but who is too often misunderstood and driven away by the barbarous and drunken mob. (II, 125.) (One remembers the Renaissance emblemata of crowds deriding poor old mendicant Homer.) This outcry against the misunderstanding and antagonism of an illiterate society is found throughout the *Poemata*. He condemns the extravagant and factious taste of the rabble in "Plebis opinio futilis" and "Populi iudicium factiosum." (II, 172; II, 247.) He condemns his century elsewhere as "seculum gustu insipido marcidum, inertique palato." (II, 137.) He observes in "A vulgo pendens"

12. Scaliger quotes Horace's compromise, "Omne tulit punctum, etc." and concurs with it in the *Poetices*, p. 285.

Qui pendet ab errore, & opinione vulgi:
Pendet magis, atq, arbore qui pendet ab alta. (II, 159.)

The tragic consequences of this lack of discrimination for the poetic profession is noted in "De poetis": ("Si haec est conditio miserae Solimane Poesis"). (I, 184.) In his "De scriptis poetarum" Scaliger tells of one of these importunate fellows with an "inert palate" who came to commission some verses; he liked the weaker pieces worthy of the vulgar throng, but as for the writings of greater value, "he spat out this madness as if it were burned honey or he were licking off a morsel stinging with salt." (I, 31-32.) Even this "rhetorical" admission that any of his verses were worthy of the throng is inconsistent; one remembers his counsel in the *Poetices libri* to reject all plebeian elements of thought or expression. "Imitate the jurisconsults who prefer to absolve ten guilty rather than condemn one innocent man—cut out ten verses rather than let one plebeian one stay."[13] No, indeed, continues Scaliger in his "Poeta," it is foolish for the poet to torture himself for three days over a single syllable, grow pale in the shadows of the theater, lock himself in the ivory tower of the temples of Sudorius—all to cater to the taste of tailors and pastrycooks. (*Poemata*, I, 80-82.) So ridiculous and pointless is the state of the poet that people who accuse him of not being a poet actually pay him a friendly tribute. How can little verses stir these Geryons who are moved by neither Zeus, Minos, or Rhadamanthus? These cicadas who chirrup against the poets are really interested only in Venus and Momus. In the past, the greatest poets from Homer, Alcman, and Orpheus on have suffered for their profession and modern society does no better: Politian died of an obscene madness, Marot starved in exile, and the "foolish filth of the mad Doletus has dried into ashes." The inclusion of Dolet here, even so described, comes as a complete surprise in view of Scaliger's belaboring of him elsewhere. Of the numerous Renaissance poets from Sidney in England to Sebastian Brant in Germany who regretted the state to which poetry had fallen, none wrote a more graphic description of the pitiable poet than Scaliger:

Tu tamen in numeris, & vano carmine perstas:
Vngues arrodis, calamo caput, & scabis aures.
Terrã oculis mera blenna voras. Tua pradia sunt haec.
Indicis somno exilium: quo stertere possis
Dum vigilas, stupidus satagis, statua aurea palles . . . (I, 80.)

13. See Eugène Lintilhac, "Jules-César Scaliger, fondateur du classicisme," *Nouvelle Revue*, LX (1890), 529.

That these complaints about the status of poets and poetry were part of a larger reaction against the cult of poetic glory we have demonstrated elsewhere.[14] Then, too, there could be moments of Christian humility, although Scaliger's Christianity was more real than his humility, when this thirst for eternal fame could be viewed as a quick-spreading poison (I, 10), or again, as "smoke and ashes after fire, a straw or flake of snow in a flame, dust on the swift southeast wind—*Solus gloria solus es, o dulcis Iesu.*" (II, 316.) This is to be compared to the rejection of "fleeting fame, lying glory, which soon dies away as the south wind" by his good friend and fellow neo-Latin, Buchanan.[15]

This thirst for fame, moreover, leads to abuses of a professional sort. "There are those whom the glory of a future fame titillates, drives, fascinates, makes anxious, burns, and urges to write." (*Poemata*, II, 140.) As a result they write hurriedly and too much, and Scaliger prescribes for them the rein rather than the spur. This advice in "Scripta praecipitata" is repeated in "Pauca parce scribere": Not everyone has the "viscera" of the swift-writing Cassius, so "Write too few things rather than too many; be scrupulous and work slowly and leisurely." (II, 201.) The thirst for fame also leads to that common indulgence of the Renaissance Orontes, mutual flattery or "sesquipedalian words" (Buchanan). Such flattery and complacency are by no means absent from the criticisms in the *Poemata*, even though drowned out in the Jovial thunderclaps which leave a more lasting resonance. But the Renaissance poets who practiced it denounced it, and Scaliger was no exception. "In mutuos laudatores" explains that these mutual admiration associations remind Scaliger of the proverb "mutuum muli scabunt." (I, 441.) A fuller development of this disapproval is contained in his satire "De mutuis laudatoribus," which he maneuvers into a weapon against Rabelais. (I, 354.) Robert Burton turned these passages back on Scaliger and his son Joseph in an ironical *obiter dictum*: "Mule scratcheth Mule, who but Scaliger with him? . . ."[16]

Ronsard, Du Bellay, and all the competent poets of the period grumbled over the superabundance of "poetasters, poetitos, parcel-poets, and poet-apes" (Swift). They even despaired, as did Jean de la Taille,[17] that with printing now so widespread, any

14. R. J. Clements, *op. cit.*, 51-77.
15. George Buchanan, *Poemata quae extant* (Lugduni Bataviae, MDCXXVIII), p. 340.
16. Robert Burton, *ed. cit.*, p. 628. See Appendix.
17. Jean de la Taille, *Art de la tragédie* (Manchester, 1939), p. 29.

fool could break into print. But no one touched off a more tremendous blast at the poetasters than did Scaliger in his "In ma-
lum poetam":

Poet more befouled than thrice-fetid goats; thou more shameless in evildoing
than timid courtiers, whether thou repeatest in your writings something novel
or the same old nonsense. Thy father is snake-devouring and thy mother a
drunken whore. He seduced her poisonously and she prostituted herself. Thou
art no poet, nor yet worthy of the coin of the furthest poet. Rather
thou must be consecrated amid the bellowing comic muses of the Arcadians,
thou whom the wild Furies splattered with their teats and Cerberus in vain
bore with his maw spuming of food. Thou didst dare, with thy poor ornament,
stammer of the fostering race of Polymnia and the pool of Pegasus. And because thou art more shameless is thine urn more drink-loving. Will all this
permit thee foolishly to think thyself a poet? That title will never re-
vert to thee. Writhe, roll round and back. Thou shalt never be numbered but
among the overseers of Tartarus.   (I, 157.)

Others in his profession trouble him. On two occasions he
condemns lying poets, though recognizing this proverbial right
of theirs ("ast mentiuntur: ast hoc est / Peculiare ac proprium
poetarum"). (II, 63; also I, 391.) He cared no more for tee-
totaling poets. In his "De poeta bibaqua" he urged poets to get
into the mood for writing with uncut wine. (I, 170.) In the
Poetices libri he acknowledged wine as a source of inspiration to
Alcman, Alcaeus, Aristophanes, Ennius, and Horace.[18] In "Ad
Musas de excellentia vini aquitanici" he granted that the Pierian
waters were all right, but that unmixed wine is preferable as an
inspiration. "But in this one little drinking cup 600 poets, I
believe, are concealed." (*Poemata*, I, 640.) This theory or motif
goes back to the rites inducing vatic furor in antiquity (*via*
Boccaccio's life of Dante, among other stages). It had contemporary pictorial expression in the emblem of Alciatus, "Vino pruden-
tiam augeri," adapted later by Schoonhovius and Peacham, and
it had gaily ironical articulation in Rabelais—"Attendez un peu
que je hume quelque traict de ceste bouteille: c'est mon vray et
seul Hélicon . . ."[19]

There are in the *Poemata* sundry other generalities about literature, including a piece on the blessings of abundant books by
this man who never left Agen except to gather up books and
manuscripts and whose vast personal library passed into the
hands of his king. ((II, 152; also I, 6.) "Scribe vacuus curis,"
as the title suggests, advises writers to ply their vocation in the

18. *Poetices*, p. 11.
19. François Rabelais, *Œuvres*, edited by Lefranc (Paris, 1931) V, 18.

morning, when they are most free from cares and Apollo shines most favorably. (II, 207.) "Misce te et versa" urges poets to put themselves into their verses and bears the counsel, "Be a mother unto thyself," quickly and sagaciously revised to "Be a step-mother unto thyself." (II, 217.)

The foregoing theory and opinion on literature reveal Scaliger as preoccupied with more or less the same issues as his contemporaries, but, because of his "apicular" and epigrammatic temperament, giving them a more vivid and exuberant expression. We turn now to Scaliger's criticisms and comments on other writers in the *Poemata*, treating first of the ancients and then of the moderns. The second section of our inquiry, immediately following, treats of Greek and Roman authors and complements the materials found in Books VI and VII of the *Poetices libri*. The third and final section of this essay will deal with Renaissance authors and will thus complement the materials in those pages of the seventh of the *Poetices libri* included under the heading of "Recentiores."

Any Aristotelian would of necessity be concerned with that notorious expulsion of the poets from Plato's theoretical *Republic*. Scaliger and his disciples endeavored to explain away this banishment in various ways, even taking the tack, as did Pinciano, that Plato wrote other passages favoring poetry which nullify this ostracizing. Among the first of the *Poemata*, "De poetis a Platone ejectis e republica" adopts the countercharge, familiar by then, that Plato himself was an imitator in words. (I, 13-14.) Hardly a word of the thousands which Plato attributed to Socrates was true and even if Plato did not merit the title of versifier, he did merit that of poet. Since poetry does not require meter or rhyme, then the very written codes which govern society and the universe are poetry. One as fearful of fictions from deceitful mouths might as well reject all memoirs and records of history.

This poem may be compared with a passage in the *Poetices libri* where Scaliger characterizes as "cruel and insensitive" those who construe Plato's *Republic* as excluding poets from the state and observes that these Platonic passages should be taken less seriously than they have been. But his feelings finally boil over: "Plato should remark how many impertinent and low stories he himself employs, what filthy thoughts this Greek rogue often forces upon us. Surely the *Symposium*, the *Phaedrus*, and other monstrous productions are not worth reading."[20] This is also the state of

20. *Poetices*, pp. 10-11.

mind in which the doctor of Agen wrote his *Contra poetices calum-niatores declamatio*, declaring that the windbag Plato should be thrown out of his own republic and denying that poetry under-mines piety or fills the mind with vices.[21] Since Scaliger dedicated his life to the propagation of the Aristotelian justifications of literature and the Ciceronian attitudes on rhetoric, he could not basically accept any general condemnation of written or oral litera-ture, even though he indulged with relish in specific condemna-tions of poets and poems. His general attitude toward Platonism impels him to write a satirical piece, "Platonis canes," deriding the militant Platonists of his time. (II, 222-23.)

Leaving aside the issue of the justification of poetry as raised by Plato, what are the specific criticisms of authors of the past in the *Poemata?* For our purposes we recall that Scaliger accepted the traditional periods of early Helladic poetry common to his century: first was that pristine and crude age out of which only the name of Apollo has survived; then came the second and venerable period when the mysteries were first sung, the age of Orpheus, Musaeus, and Linus; last came the great age of Homer and Hesiod.[22]

The only poet of the first two periods to receive an exclusive tribute was Apollo. A splendid ode to this first singer ("Aurei plenum meditantis ictum") recalls the magic and therapeutic powers of Apollo's song, pacifying beasts, subduing warriors, and even calming the waters of the sea:

> Uber arguto saliens fluento
> Fistula arridet. trepidumque puro
> Gestiens riuo fluuius canoras
> Temperat undas. (*Poemata*, I, 172.)

It was no secret even to his contemporaries that Scaliger's ver-giliolatry made him unusually critical of Homer. In the *Poetices libri* he devoted many pages to a comparison of these epicists, find-ing that Homer was to Vergil as a meager pastor's snack is to a feast in the king's palace. There is one conventionally laudatory piece, "Homerus," in the *Poemata* which apparently dates from as early as 1539. "No human beings, no Muses brought me forth, but from me as father the Muses took their origin." (I, 329.) And in his undated *Declamatio* he recalls Horace's admiration of Homer and deems Homer worthy of study. Yet even in the *Poemata* the attack on Homer is echoed. In the poem on Plato's

---

21. See Vernon Hall, "Scaliger's Defense of Poetry," *PMLA*, LXI (1948), 1125-30.

22. *Poetices*, p. 11.

banishment of poets, he exonerates Plato for expelling from his state the "subversive" Homer, "composing the jests which he established as precepts for poets, fictions and evil crimes he attributed to the gods, and struggles of heroes enacted with a foul madness of confusion." (I, 13.) Scaliger is generally granted a major role in the discrediting of Homer in the sixteenth and seventeenth centuries. "Mais c'est Scaliger, dans son *Art poétique*, qui inaugure la mode, triomphante au 17e siècle, qui consiste à incriminer les fautes du goût, les trivialités, les péchés contre les règles dont se rendit coupable Homère. Pour Scaliger Virgile est Dieu, et les Latins surpassent les Grecs."[23] True, whereas in the first preface to the *Franciade* Ronsard seems to place Homer and Vergil on equal footing, in the second Homer is scarcely mentioned.[24] Scaliger's feeling that Homer lacked the taste and elegance of Vergil was a condemnation not only of Homer, but of the society in which Homer lived, of which he wrote, and which found him acceptable.[25]

Aristotle, viewed as an eagle soaring over crows, is praised in passing for his rhetoric. (II, 174.) Plato and Aristotle of course receive a poetic accolade among the others of the section *Heroes*. Aristotle is praised as "penes Deos homo, penes homines Deus." (I, 314.) Improvising upon the Platonic cosmography, Scaliger decides that his own poems need not extol Plato to the skies, since Plato has already accomplished this ascension to the upper sphere through his genius and tongue. (I, 315.) A tercet on Aristotle, Plato, and Isocrates turns out to be a pronouncement on the gradual corruption of the Greek language. "Macedonian speech is like a timid maiden; to this the member of the Academy foolishly added the element of high color; while that of Isocrates may be compared to that of a shameless harlot." (II, 174.) This Isocrates is certainly a contrast to the Isocrates in the *Poetices libri* who is credited therein with putting the graceful finishing touches on what had been before him a rude vehicle of diction and expression.[26]

In his *Poetices libri*, Scaliger was unappreciative of the primitive grandeur of Aeschylus. To understand his censure of Aeschylus one needs to remember that tragic playwrights must portray

23. Marcel Raymond, *L'Influence de Ronsard* (Paris, 1927), I, 326.

24. Noted *inter alia* in F. Brunetière, *L'Evolution des genres* (Paris, 1922), pp. 51-52.

25. See the discussion in Vernon Hall, *Life of Scaliger, ed. cit.*, p. 153.

26. *Poetices*, p. 285.

historical events authentically, having the license only to adapt the action and speeches to the characters.[27] Thus, mindful also of the "unity of time," he can write in his poetic art: "Most men find mendacity to their dislike. That is why those battles and sieges at Thebes which are over in two hours displease me. No scrupulous poet would make anyone move from Delphi to Thebes or Thebes to Athens in a moment's time. Agamemnon is buried by Aeschylus after being killed off, without leaving the actor time to breathe. Nor can anyone approve of Hercules' casting Lichas into the sea, since this violates truth."[28] Scaliger's poem "Vaecordia veterum poetarum" indicts Aeschylus on these same grounds of verisimilitude and historicity. He finds it hard to swallow the events in the *Oresteia* after the slaying of Clytemnestra, such events as the vengeance of the Erinyes. (*Poemata*, II, 224.)

Other Greek writers pass in hasty review. A poem to Pindar is a vehicle for manipulating such conventional imagery as Pegasus, swans, and such tropes as were dear to Pindar's heart. (I, 326.) Xenophon's great chronicle of Cyrus was worthy of Pallas and the Pythian themselves. (I, 327.) Scaliger portrays the charming natural setting in which the gracious odes of Sappho originated, including:

> Blandus Amor, mitis tellus, lenissimus aurae
> Tractus, dant Sappho dulcia scripta tibi. (I, 383.)

We recall the pun in the poetics about Anacreon's introducing not only *melos* but *mel* in his songs when a stanza to Anacreon tells of his honeyed vein. (I, 332.) An entire section in the *Poemata* falls under the heading of *Anacreontica*, while another section title is *Archilochus*. Scaliger admires the sententiae in Euripides, finding to his taste such pithy questions as "utrum vivere mors, vita mors sit?" (II, 179-80).

If we have been led to expect that Scaliger's preference for Roman language, literature, and society will win easy approval of Roman writers, we are discounting Scaliger's congenital severity. Lucretius is mentioned noncommittally in the *Poetices libri* as a poet of natural philosophy as opposed to moral philosophy; in the *Poemata* Scaliger attacks and ridicules Lucretius' doctrine of the absence of design and purpose in nature, even while continuing to revere the Roman writer's great poetic strength, mastery of meter, and "fireborn madness." (I, 12.)

27. *Ibid.*, p. 12.
28. *Ibid.*, p. 368.

The second Roman poet mentioned in the *Poemata* is Ovid, and the strophe is in the form of an invective, or even malediction, penned to Augustus by Ovid from his exile along the Black Sea, whither he had been banished by a king who, as E. K. Rand pointed out, simply did not read him in the right frame of mind. Ovid is made to express regret that he has written a poem (in the Getic language) praising the emperor, and to ventilate several grievances. The opening verses set the tone:

> A me utinam inciperes ferus esse cruente: nec atras
>   Per caedes faceres ad mea fata gradum.
> Si mea te movit tetricum lasciva iuventus:
>   Te iuvenem damnas perditus: exul abi.
> Impia flagitiis squallent penetralia diris.
>   Damnati superant nomina foeda rei, *etc.* (I, 328.)

The relations between Cicero and Camillus, like those between Ovid and Augustus, offered Scaliger the chance for dramatic soliloquy on Cicero's political participations on behalf of freedom; he rises to the vigorous and lofty tone of the Ciceronian *Philippics* against Mark Anthony.

> Heu patriae cineres, patriae o morientis imago:
> Non poteram non, iam te moriente mori. (I, 336.)

One of Scaliger's *apiculae*, "Cicero in Lyceo," reminds us that Cicero is the paragon and model of pure speech for the learner (II, 25-26), a small footnote to the vigorous orations defending Cicero against Erasmus.[29]

That hoary and archaic Ennius (if one believes the Renaissance humanists, Ennius was, like Confucius, already aged at birth) receives a solemn accolade befitting his primitive gravity:

> Magne senex, cui torva graui sonat horrida cantu
> Buccina bellaci cum crepat hasta manu, *etc.* (I, 325.)

We have already referred to the apotheosis of Vergil in the *Poetices libri*, where his words are judged worthy of a god and he is hailed as the god of poets. This upward sweep through the spheres is suggested by the favorite Renaissance epithet of "Phoenix," applied to him in the *Poemata* (II, 174), and by the assertion that whereas Mantua and Calabria claim him, this great epic poet has transcended the earth itself. (I, 336).

Julius Caesar, as author of the *Commentaries*, is likened to an eagle and praised by his namesake: " Caesar creperi gloria, fulmen

29. See above, note 7.

atque belli." (II, 174.) In another place Scaliger announces that
he will write in "a pure Latin free from blemishes, like that of
Caesar and Terence." (I, 422.) Horace never occupies the stage
in the *Poemata*, not even in the succession of *Heroes*, a fact which
gains in significance when one recalls that Scaliger called the
epistle to the Pisos an art of poetry without art and made it clear
that he preferred the tractates of Aristotle and Vida.[30]

That Scaliger would prefer among all the magnificent writers
of the Renaissance those who clung to Latin is already adumbrated
in the *Poetices libri*, where Fracastoro was rated the major poet of
the "recentiores," with Vida and Sannazaro at his heels. This pre-
judice must be kept in mind as one studies Scaliger's comments
on his contemporaries. It must also be remembered that a complete perquisition of Scaliger's views on his contemporaries is made
difficult by the number of praises or censures in which the re-
cipients are veiled under such comic names as Bambalio, Furnellus,
Struma, and so on. Some of these allusions were comprehensible
to his contemporaries or to the recipient, but others must have remained his own private jokes. Finally, one must not forget that
Scaliger lived in the golden age of the literary feud, with antagonists springing up out of dragons' teeth (as Alciatus phrased it)[31]
in each major country: Nash *vs.* Harvey, Lope *vs.* Góngora,
Sagon *vs.* Marot, Castelvetro *vs.* Annibal Caro, and so on.

Scaliger, who had started his career as a warrior in the armies
of the Emperor Maximilian, became an armchair general in the
literary warfare of his time. He initiated at least four feuds himself—with Rabelais, Dolet, Cardan, and Erasmus. Scaliger was
never more militant than against Dolet, whose very name he toys
with mercilessly in his *Logogriphi*. (I, 629.) There are a number
of barbed poems directed at this humanist and translator who had
sought Scaliger's friendship, but against whom Scaliger sided in
Dolet's feud with Pinachius.[32] When Scaliger hears that Dolet
has been complimented as a sort of sturdy oak of literature,
he notes that there is many a Sillotimone, Laelius, and Aristide
who would like to wield the axe. Dolet is more like the pests which
infest trees: gnawing worms, drone bees, leek killers, and roaches
which eat the leaves. (I, 403.) A short epigrammatic outburst
which does no particular credit to Scaliger harps on the theme
that being Dolet and being a poet are two distinct things, and

---

30. See section on "Scaligers Abhängigkeit von Horaz" in Brinkschulte.
31. Andreas Alciatus, *Emblèmes* (Lyon, 1564), p. 228.
32. See V. Hall, *Life of Scaliger*, pp. 106-7.

demonstrates how tiresome six lines of abuse can become. (I, 194-95.)

Although the humanistic writers of the time were campaigning for enrichment and "illustration" of the vernacular language through translation and innutrition, Scaliger was such a neo-Latin at heart that he begrudged Dolet's efforts in this direction. He devotes two poems to Dolet's translations from Latin writers. In the first of these, "De libris quos inscripsit Doletus Fata Francisci Regis," Scaliger begins scornfully, "Because he believes that things vainly plagiarized from the Tullian books are permitted to be circulated among his trifling works, well, the one who brings back the feather of Aesop's jackdaw thought the same thing." (I, 409.) When Dolet lifts as few as four verses from Maro at one time, a negligible amount of "imitation" in those days, Scaliger points at them as at a gold ornament or a scarlet flower on the plagiarist's garment. On another page Dolet becomes a Terentian eunuch who aims at many things, but excels in few. (I, 429-430) Dolet dips at will into the Tullian source and appropriates whatever he pleases. Scaliger's language takes on that vivid, precipitous quality and cumulative effect which mark his best invective. Dolet copies also from the Greeks:

> Idem videri Graeca scire contendit.
> Ast illa nouit, vt rigare de flamma,
> Sudare sub Biarnico polo nudus.
> Aures tamen fatigat, & necat scriptis,
> Quae pro suis deprompta de penu Scaevae
> Torquet, retorquet.

There are, of course, other barbs in which Dolet remained incognito. Scaliger wrote to Arnoul Le Ferron about Dolet, "I tongue-lashed him in my second discourse [the *Oratio in eundum* of 1535] although without naming him, but I painted him in such a way that the children of Toulouse would recognize him even in tights." The whole unpleasant feud between Scaliger and Dolet has been interestingly related in Charles Nisard's *Les Gladiateurs de la république des lettres*.[33]

François Rabelais was a worthy antagonist endowed with that most deadly arm of defense, a sense of humor. He had apparently studied medicine under Scaliger at Agen and incurred the latter's dislike by preferring as medical mentor Jean Schyron. The feud became so bitter that Rabelais denounced Scaliger to Erasmus as a

33. Charles Nisard, *Les Gladiateurs de la république des lettres* (Paris, 1860).

godless slanderer.[34] The undoubtedly witty ripostes of Rabelais
have not been preserved, but the *Poemata* are riddled with epigrammatic pieces against Baryoenus or Rabioenus, the pseudonym
of Rabelais, as De Santi informed us back in 1905.[35] Scaliger
attacked François as a twice defrocked monk and as a friend of
Dolet. His stanza beginning "Hic domita ossa piis Baryoeni sunt
sita flammis" registers the canards which began to circulate about
Rabelais after his death. It reads, "The vanquished mortal remains
of Baryoenus are now the prey of pious flames. Water was unable
to decompose the cadaver of this frightful criminal; it is a dog
which has gnawed him away. God was far away at the time. And
why? Because there was not the slightest bit of God in him."
(I, 194.) Rabelais was not only a defrocked monk, but also an
atheist, not even worth those corpses which at least fertilize the
barren fields. (I, 151; also I, 215.) Rabelais, as we have seen,
repaid in kind for this charge of atheism. In two other pieces
Scaliger ridicules the epigrams which Rabelais directs back at him.
Rabelais' humor is intended for the bumpkins of the crossroads
and the public market and François is grief-stricken that he cannot
equal the "iambs" of Scaliger. Scaliger defends himself from
Rabelais' charge that he is neglecting his medical duties to
become a poor and pale scrivener. (I, 350; I, 216; see also the
three attacks on this human Cerberus in I, 194.) This defense is
better undertaken in the poem "Quare versus faciat," summarized
above. Many more "iambs" disguise Rabelais under the pseudonym of Bibinus and attack him as a dipsomaniac, a reputation
which Rabelais gained in his lifetime as much through his writings
as through intemperance. (I, 356, 450, 451, 455, and *passim.*)

   Although he remained aloof from such *ralliements* as the
Pléiade or the Lyonese group, Scaliger admired their devotion to
classical literature, to which some of them had been introduced by
Jean Dorat, considered by Scaliger the most judicious critic and
most able establisher of texts in the century.[36] The poem "Scripsit
haec pro poetis Gallicanis" praises the new brigade of poets
springing forth in the Loire and Garonne valleys. This poem, better known than others in the *Poemata*, has occasionally been quoted
as proof that Scaliger did, after all, approve and commend the
innovations and reforms of the Pléiade. He singles out the group
of Ronsard and Jodelle as a "wondrous generation which have

34. The letter to Erasmus is translated in Hall, *Life*, p. 107.
35. See above, note 6.
36. Henri Chamard, *Joachim du Bellay* (Lille, 1900), p. 52.

equalled the power of the remote generations." (I, 205.) And elsewhere in the *Poemata* he apostrophizes Ronsard as "blazing in his light and eclipsing Anacreon" (I, 472), permitting us to date this period of admiration as being shortly after 1555, when the *Continuation des amours* rejected Pindar in favor of Anacreon. Since Scaliger died in 1558, this late recognition of Ronsard was merely the late recognition of an accomplished fame. But the poem on behalf of the Gallic poets praises those on the Garonne as well as the Loire; these were Buchanan in Bordeaux and Vulteius at Toulouse further up the river, two neo-Latin poets utterly disinterested in the generic, prosodic, and linguistic aims of the Pléiade. The force of this tribute to the Pléiade is further weakened by an effusive tribute in the *Poemata* to that mocker of the Pléiade, Mellin de Saint-Gelays, epitome of the flaccid court poetry decried by the Pléiade. (I, 167.)

Most of the Pléiade group did not attack the celebrated stargazer and writer of prophecies, Nostradamus, physician at Agen and medical disciple of Scaliger. Ronsard even claimed that his prophecies were coming true.[37] Scaliger, despite his own propensity for prophetic visions,[38] found Nostradamus an easy target for his bolts. He aims and writes:

> Si Nostradamus, quid pudere sit, nescit:
> Quod est paratum, nec reconditum, & praesens,
> Quanam futura notione mentitur? (I, 447.)

He scoffs at Nostradamus' alleged descent from the prophets of Benjamin, adding that Michel would have been twice as good a prophet had he been descended from Mahomet. (I, 199.) A final outburst against Nostradamus' "babbling" reads:

> Credula quid speras: quid spectas pendula verbis
> Gallia, Iudaea quae blatit arte furor? (I, 222.)

The wording of this last question would indicate that Scaliger had not forgotten that Nostradamus, Pierre Turel, and their confreres were the product of the prophetic furor which Ficino and the neo-Platonists (like Plato himself in the *Phaedrus*) considered cogeneric with the poetic fury. Scaliger's epidorpidian verse "Astrologi" sees the belief in astrologers as resulting from the "leaden stupidity" of the public. (II, 239.)

A number of neo-Latins among his Italian contemporaries now pass in review. Fracastoro, ranked as outstanding in the *Poetices*

---

37. Pierre de Ronsard, *Œuvres complètes* (Paris, 1914-19), V, 360.
38. See Hall, *Life*, p. 123.

libri, is again praised as a modern classic, favored by Apollo and "ingens" as a doctor and as a poet. (I, 324.) This extravagant feeling was not colored by personal acquaintance, by the way. To Sadoletus, who adopted Latin in both his learned treatises and his poetry and who, like Scaliger, tried to reconcile the extremes of religious thinking in his day, the man who defended Cicero against Erasmus expressed the goal:

> Haec summa est: recte sapere, & bene dicere verum.
> Sic solus iunxi cum Cicerone Deum. (I, 312.)

That Pontanus, the neo-Latin of the Neapolitan group, should have dedicated himself to poetry when he was so capable in other fields ("quot quantas attigit artes") surprises Scaliger. "No one ever treated better the prizes of peace, or strong hand teach justice by the sword. No court ever heard a better tongue, nor sober table better jokes." (I, 324.)

Politian and Pico della Mirandola receive dutiful but uncritical tribute among the *Heroes*. (I, 316.) Scaliger is grateful to Bembo for being the most devoted Ciceronian in Italy and records this fact:

> Si probitas, pietas, grauitas, animusq, quietus
> Cedunt iis numeris, qui Ciceronis erant:
> Sic palmam ex Cicerone feram, sin gloria maior
> Ex illis palmam de Cicerone feram. (I, 317.)

Bandello, who lived for a while in Agen (of all places!) and became an intimate of Scaliger, receives conventional applause as a singer of love (I, 327); another tribute exploits the Pindaric notion that his amores to Lucrezia Gonzaga raise both the poet and his mistress to the skies. (I, 173-74.) Bandello is thus one of the few writers in the vernacular praised by Scaliger. Another is Mario Equicola, author of the popular *Libro di natura di amore* ("Atque pares fausto condis amore iocos"). (I, 533.) Scaliger considers the *bacia* of Johannes Secundus "gentle, sweet, smooth, languid," and so on. (I, 197.) He finds that Ficino's exegeses and translations of Plato were works of virtue which lifted Marsilio in a Platonic ascension right up to the rarefied realm above the Angelic Mind. Of Ficino's soul he exclaims:

> Ter caeli socia es: ter magni civis olympi:
> Ter comes in gremium pulchra recepta, Dei. (I,333.)

The charming Vittoria Colonna, neo-Platonic poetess of Rome, is praised among the *Heroinae*, but no allusion is made to her *Rime*.

To achieve the transition from Italian to French writers there is Marguerite d'Angoulême, not unlike her correspondent, Vittoria Colonna, in many ways. But Scaliger makes no reference to her *Heptaméron* or her abundant literary production, although he appears to recall in passing the mystical spirit which infuses the *Prisons* ("te solum te Christe petens, tua vincula plangens"). (I, 462.) In one passage Scaliger has high praise for the young Etienne de la Boétie (I, 20-21), but on two other occasions he worries that this brilliant youth, caught between law and poetry, will cast aside his creative talent. (I, 420, 423-24; also *Poetices*, p. 150.) Scaliger has a boundless admiration for his friend Buchanan, Scotsman turned Frenchman, whom he calls "god of the critics." When Buchanan requests to see some poemata, Scaliger becomes almost reverent and abject: "Why should you request to hear me, with my rough, inharmonious, and barbarous voice, full of nonsense and absurd in my unbearable artifice? When Apollo plies the plectrum, will Marsyas try a stroke of his thumb? If Thalia compose her lovable measures, will the magpie exult in babbling?" (I, 178.)

Far more patently sincere is the fine stanza written to Andreas Melanchthon, nephew of Philip Melanchthon, in the dungeon at Château Trompette. Scaliger commends this personal friend, who has been accused of heresy, for his fortitude. "We grieve that thou art being held in the worst of evils: grief, illness, prison, thirst, and hunger." (I, 167.) Scaliger adds that he is dedicating all of his current labors to the release of his friend. Apparently sincere is his stanza deploring the death of Erasmus, with whom he had tried to pick a literary quarrel in 1531 and 1536.[39] He asks Erasmus why he left this earth before Scaliger's affection could be made more acceptable to him, praises the Olympian thunderbolts of Erasmus' mind and tongue, and stands frightened before the realization that the greatest divinities can die. (I, 323.)

The preceding pages bring to light theory, imagery, and criticism which contribute to a broader understanding of Scaliger as a thinker on the "more humane" letters. There are facets of his theory which do not show up elsewhere: the notion of artistic compulsion, the disillusions about the vocation of poetry, and so on. There are facets of his criticism which modify or contradict ideas presented in the *Poetices libri*: his deprecation of the diction and language of Isocrates, his early adulation of Homer, and so on. After the labored objectivity of the *Poetices libri*, the *Poemata*

39. *Lettres françaises inédites de Joseph Scaliger* (Agen, 1879), pp. 324-25.

reveal bases of judgment—personal, ethical, and social—assuming considerable importance in his critical thinking. Scaliger had, after all, prepared himself in philosophy and theology as well as medicine at Bologna and Padua. The *Poemata* show a greater versatility at the "working level" of this thinking. The exuberance and abundance of superlatives in the *Poemata* are matched by extravagant improvising upon the themes of inspiration. If these superlatives sometimes become meaningless, if Scaliger sometimes disappoints us by recourse to unqualified, unexplained praise or censure, leaving our curiosity unsatisfied concerning the criteria behind the judgment, if indeed any criteria are present at all, he makes up for this on a few occasions by his total immersion in the spirit of the writer under scrutiny. Thus the elevated tone of the philippic he places in the mouth of his Cicero, the impassioned malediction which he pens for his Ovid, or the neo-Platonism which infuses his praises of Plato and Marsilio Ficino all capture so well the spirit of the authors in question that we know them to be favorite reading of the scholar of Agen and we know what it was about them which impressed him. His notorious preference for Romans over Greeks is partially substantiated by the *Poemata*, for in them he speaks ill of Homer, Plato, Aeschylus, and Isocrates, while only dissenting on a point of natural philosophy with Lucretius.

On the other hand, to keep our perspective we must see that Scaliger did have sincere praise for Aristotle, Pindar, Anacreon, Xenophon, Euripides, Sappho, and even on occasion for Homer and Plato. His known preference for neo-Latins or "recentiores" over writers in the vernacular is almost totally confirmed by the *Poemata*. Almost every writer of the Renaissance who wrote in the vernacular and nevertheless won his praise turns out to be a personal acquaintance or correspondent of his: Bandello, La Boétie, Mellin de Saint-Gelays, Marguerite d'Angoulême, and even Ronsard and Jodelle. All the rest, whether Italian, French, or British, are of the late Latinity. In fact, Rabelais and Dolet added insult to injury by their espousal of the vernacular language. His preference for the neo-Latins is evident not only from his almost exclusive attention to them, but from his unflinching praise of them. Not one is censured in the *Poemata*, not even Erasmus. And yet many a writer in the vernacular is passed over in silence. Not even Dante or Petrarch is mentioned. But then, typical of the period of the Pléiade, Scaliger failed entirely to see the greatness of mediaeval literature. He was equally blind to the "new swans" singing on the other side of the Pyrenees, the English Channel, and the Rhine. Yet this did not prevent his influence from becoming tremendous in those neighboring countries. Pinciano suggested to his reader that after he had finished his own thirteen books of poetics he should then start on Scaliger,[40] and Henry Peacham called the "divine" Scaliger "the prince of all learning and the judge of judgments."[41]

We cannot determine the periods when most of the *Poemata* were written. Some were composed as early as 1535, but we have found that the stanza to the "Anacreontic" Ronsard must date from the last two or three years of Scaliger's life. The "epidorpidian" inedita were gathered together by his son Joseph (who defined their title as meaning *reliefs* or *rogatons*: scraps and scrapings) at the last minute for the 1561 edition. Since we know little if any more about the exact periods of composition of the *Poetices libri septem*, it is difficult to utilize the treatise and the poetry to establish progressions in Scaliger's thinking. Aristotelian neoclassicism advocated consistency in thinking, and indeed assumed it as a natural consequence of reliance upon logic and reason. Since everything points to a static quality in the neoclassic Scaliger's thinking, the question of the evolution of his ideas becomes less important in him than in a Ronsard.

In the *Poemata* it is disturbing to perceive how wanting in humanity and how boring some of the invective can be. Granted that "the humanists were not a happy family"[42] and that the stinging epigram, iambic, and satire were accepted literary forms in the Renaissance, there seems to be little reason for Scaliger to have continued his scurrilities against Dolet after Dolet had been sent to the pyre in 1546. After all, Scaliger himself had been brought before the Inquisition eight years earlier on the same charge that sent Dolet to his death in the Place Maubert: the state and whereabouts of the soul after death. Nor was there much reason for the moralistic stabbing of a dead Rabelais († 1553). Chronologies do not even permit us to explain this abuse of other religious "subversives" as a mechanism of self-defense. He was, as Robert Burton observed, more wrathful than Archilochus, who

---

40. López Pinciano, *Philosophía antigua poética* (Madrid, 1950), I, 9-10; Pinciano also rates him as "muy bueno y sobre todos auentajado."

41. Quoted in J. E. Spingarn, *Literary Criticism in the Renaissance* (New York, 1912), p. 310.

42. C. H. C. Wright, *History of French Literature* (New York, 1912), p. 143, deals with this aspect of Scaliger.

had obviously inspired his invectives.[43] It was the Scaliger temperament which incited Alciatus to include among his emblemata a plate showing a swallow snatching in his beak a singing cicada, symbol of one poet dying from another's bite.[44] But this satirical and hostile approach to writers of obvious merit hurt Scaliger as well as his victims. It was as Scaliger's compatriot Baudoin wrote, "Ces pointes d'esprit, que l'on appelle bons mots, produisent souvent de fort mauvais effects, & sont plus nuisibles à ceux qui les disent, qu'à ceux qui les souffrent pour un temps, & dont le Temps aussi les venge à la fin."[45] Indeed, counterattacks and libels of a virulent sort ensued, usually protecting themselves with that very anonymity with which Scaliger had veiled his victims. At one point it was feared that his enemies were sending cloak and dagger agents to Agen to kill him.[46] And even an intimate friend like his admiring and admired Vulteius turned against this "Zoilus armed with mad iambics" for his hammering blows at Rabelais.[47] Despite all this, a reading of the *Poemata* reveals a wealth of unpublicized comment and criticism which are as extreme in their praise of other writers as the more publicized attacks are extreme in their vituperation.

Julius Caesar Scaliger is generally accepted, in Lintilhac's phrase, as "le fondateur du classicisme" in France and he is credited with having established, a full century before Boileau, the cult of rational neo-classicism. In his now famous essay, "Qu'est-ce qu'un classique?", Sainte-Beuve defines classicism as "cette théorie qui subordonne l'imagination et la sensibilité elle-même à la raison et dont Scaliger peut-être a donné le premier signal chez les modernes."[48] And Raymond summarizes, "Grâce à lui, la coutume s'établit d'emprisonner la poésie dans les catégories de la raison. . . . Il représentait le bon sens vigoureux, le rationalisme à vues limitées."[49] It is certainly true that Scaliger entertained no doubts about his theories being the product of logic and reason, nor about himself as the voice of reason in his applied

43. See Appendix.

44. Andreas Alciatus, *Emblemata* (Paris, 1589): item: "Doctus doctis obliqui nefas esse."

45. I. Baudoin, *Recueil d'emblèmes divers* (Paris, 1647): item: "Que les querelles entre gens de lettres sont mal-séantes."

46. *Lettres françaises inédites de Joseph Scaliger, ed. cit.*, pp. 82-83.

47. Quoted in Hall, *Life*, p. 115.

48. Sainte-Beuve, *Causeries du lundi* (1851-72), III, 44.

49. Marcel Raymond, *op. cit.*, I, 326.

criticisms.[50] Long before Boileau's famous "Aimez donc la raison" and his exaltation of the golden mean, Scaliger anticipated him with the following literary credo:

In controversis medium seco, iudico parcus:
Nec mihi, sed rationi: aut quod ratio esse videtur.   (I, 10.)

50. To establish the consistency of thinking between Julius Caesar Scaliger and his phenomenally learned son, Joseph Justus Scaliger, the reader should compare the contents of this article with George W. Robinson's "Joseph Scaliger's Estimates of Greek and Latin Authors," *Harvard Studies in Classical Philology,* XXIX (1918), 135-36.

V

LOPEZ PINCIANO'S *PHILOSOPHIA ANTIGUA POETICA* AND THE SPANISH CONTRIBUTION TO RENAISSANCE LITERARY THEORY

S PAIN has been consistently disregarded by those historians who have devoted books to comparative literary theory in the humanistic period, from Saintsbury and Spingarn down to such recent investigators as Vernon Hall. It has been commonly accepted that the sweep of neoclassical theory in literature and art crossed from Italy to France and thence to England, leaving scarcely a trace in such bypaths as Germany, Spain and Portugal. The notorious peninsularity of so many Spanish writers on the *europeización de España* has led most students of comparative criticism and aesthetics to believe that Spain's contribution in this area was negligible until "enfin Luzán vint." Indeed, we possess a history of literary criticism in Spain from Luzán to the present, by Fernández y González, but none from the origins to Luzán. We have only one volume of the rich but unsystematic *Historia de las ideas estéticas* of Menéndez y Pelayo to make us aware that materials exist for a systematic study of Renaissance literary theory in Spain.

The Siglo de Oro writers themselves did not help matters by their own deprecation of themselves as theorists. Lope's characterization of the neoclassic canons as "el arte que conocen pocos" and his exclusion of them "con seis llaves" are well known, even though Lope observed these canons to a greater extent than he admitted or perhaps realized. At the end of the sixteenth century, sixty years after Aristotle was first vernacularized, no pleiad had formed in Spain to propagate neoclassic literary theory. What poetic arts had been composed were unknown to the Spaniards themselves. In 1596 López Pinciano finds no poetic art in his country and sets out to write one: "Sabe Dios ha muchos años desseo ver un libro desta materia sacado a luz de mano de otro por no me poner hecho señal y blanco de las gentes, y sabe que por ver mi patria, florecida en todas las demás disciplinas, estar en esta parte tan falta y necessitada, determiné a arriscar por la socorrer" (Carballo edition, I, 8). True, there had been little more than Alfonso X's rhetoric ridden *Setenario*, the brief paragraphs of the Marqués de Santillana, the *Consistorio del*

Gay Saber of Luis de Averró and Jaime March, and the sketchy *Arte* of Juan del Encina.

The question poses itself whether and how a great literature ("florecida") can arise and flourish without being sustained by a theoretic and a consciousness of purpose. It has been stated that the hegemony of Italian Renaissance literature and art resulted from the abundantly articulated theory which underlay them. A contrary school of thought holds that theory and practice are divorced. In his *Cycles of Taste*, Chambers finds that Hellenic art was great in the absence of any conscious aesthetic. Similarly, it has been thought that the greatness of Siglo de Oro literature was the product not of an aesthetic self-consciousness, but of an independent creativeness."... sin arte Rhetórica ni Poética podría auer hombres que las entendiessen," declared Pinciano, "... sin Poética ay poetas" (III, 228).

It is gradually becoming clear that this second school of thought is not valid for Renaissance Spain and that there was a theoretic supporting Siglo de Oro literature. Lope de Vega, author of *comedias* which were neither comedies nor tragedies in the neoclassic sense, had his theorist in Pinciano, who testified "yo he visto en comedias muy finas y puras muchos temores, llantos y aun muertes" (III, 22) and saw clearly that the distinction between comedies and tragedies was one of spirit and not of such incidentals as happy or sad endings: "Pues las tragedias también suelen tener alegres fines." His analysis of comedy, tragedy, and tragicomedy championed Spanish dramatists over two centuries before Alcalá Galiano's preface to *El moro expósito*. Incidentally establishing the existence of this early corpus of theory, the Spaniards are beginning to make available their most important Renaissance poetic arts, thanks to the Consejo Superior de Investigaciones Científicas. The Consejo has brought out the *Arte poética en romance castellano* (1580) of Sánchez de Lima, a dialogued "defense and illustration" of Spanish verse and language; the *Libro de la erudición poética* (1596) of Luis Carrillo de Sotomayor, a sententious and learned repertory of ancient and conventional theory; and finally, the *Philosophía antigua poética* (1611) of Alonzo López Pinciano, spaciously and carefully reprinted by Alfredo Carballo Picazo (Madrid, 1953). To this corpus of theory Espasa-Calpe have made available Juan de Cueva's *Ejemplar poético* (Madrid, 1953) as they had Lope's *Arte nuevo*.

The reappearance of Pinciano's dialogue was a major event, for it is one of the most complete and rewarding poetic treatises

in the Renaissance. A physician, like Aristotle (and Apollo: 1, 8),
Pinciano set himself the goal of elucidating Aristotle. For him
and his generation it was not Lope but rather the Stagirite who
was the "monstruo de naturaleza" (III, 121). The greatness
of Pinciano is that he coupled as tenaciously analytical a mind as
his fellow medic Julius Caesar Scaliger with as practical a sense
of the realities of verse and theater as Castelvetro or Lope. Few
theorists in the Renaissance who had the patience to trace the
occurrence of minor figures of speech through Greek and Latin
literature could become equally engrossed in the relative effective-
ness of actors' foot or eye movements on the stage or in the
question of how many entrances and exits an actor should make
in a five-act play.

This versatile mind was torn between the necessity of giving
Spain a formal articulation and exegesis of the questions raised
by Aristotle and the realization, unusual for Pinciano's time, that
the limits of criticism and aesthetics must be enlarged to en-
compass issues which were never envisioned by Aristotle. To ex-
tend the frontiers of Renaissance criticism, he familiarizes himself with accessible Greek and Roman philosophers and critics.
His analyses of such eternal issues as katharsis (I, 176), poetic
fury (I, 227), obscurity (II, 160), and the essence of laughter
(III, 33) are among the most comprehensive known to the
Renaissance. He was likewise one of the most forward-looking
theorists of his age. He anticipates the seventeenth century with
his discussion of the *"merveilleux chrétien,"* which as a classicist
he opposes (II, 67); the eighteenth century with his discussion of
the "paradox of the comedian": "Será bien que el trágico mueua
a llanto sin llorar él" (III, 283); and the nineteenth century
with his remarks on local color (III, 278), which he rightly views
as an extension of the neoclassic issue of verisimilitude. His com-
prehensiveness leads him to speculations on the relationships between poetry and philosophy (I, 220), music (III, 103), art (I,
169, etc.), medicine (III, 261), and many another discipline.

His defense of creative literature against its traditional antagonists, the historians, philosophers, and churchmen, is consistent and subtle in a country which produced the militant force
of the Counter-Reformation but never needed a Counter- Reformation itself. Pinciano's role of defender carries him so far as to
clear Plato of the charge of being against poets: "no se deue creer
que un varón como Platón . . . contradiga injustamente a lo que
justamente dixo antes, y diga mal de la poesía, ni de los poetas

en general" (I, 165); and "amó mucho a la Poética" (I, 180). He consistently denies the proverbial charge of mendacity on the part of poets, justifying poetry as imitation. The theater especially needed apologists. Like Voltaire much later, he is indignant that people should wish to exclude actors from the sacrament of the Eucharist and burial in hallowed ground: "Si la poesía . . . es obra honesta y vtil en el mundo, ¿por qué el que la pone en ejecución será vil y infame?" (III, 264). But the precaution of a sort of *trompe-l'œil* is necessary. Poetry is by nature good and veracious, but if there are bad and mendacious poets, of course they harm society. After analyzing an anticlerical joke, Pinciano's friend Fadrique hastily adds, "Todos los religiosos son muy buenos y castos" (III, 66). And while the theater is patently a good influence, there are histrions and *zarabandistas* (cf. III, 93) who are harmful to morals and to the welfare of the state. Pinciano even wonders for the record whether censorship may not be a necessary control (III, 273).

By casting in dialogue form his *theórica* (for Pinciano, *poética* served as often as not as synonym for *poesía*), Don Alfonso responded to a need of his inquiring mind to approach problems from different sides. Thus his work is divided into thirteen epistles recording as many dialogues (more properly, trialogues) held between the bookish doctor and his two neighbors, the Valencian Fadrique and his fellow-physician Ugo, all of them curious, enthusiastic, and fond of argument. Frequently this framework lets one participant uphold the thesis, another the antithesis, with a third present to voice any possible synthesis. In this *summa* the literary issues become incarnate. Ugo can insist upon the glorious rewards of the poetic profession while Pinciano can emphasize the disadvantages (I, 153-155). Fadrique can play the Platonist to Ugo's Aristotelianism (I, 167, 202). Fadrique can prefer tragedy on grounds of nobility and Ugo can prefer the epic (III, 205). The dialogue form affords liveliness and humor and allows for the brief stage setting which characterized neo-Platonic colloquies. Two *picaras* singing saucy songs lead the shocked trio to a discussion of dithyrambic poetry. A trip to the Teatro de la Cruz to see a performance of *Iphigenia* leads to a discussion of the theater. All the tempests of contemporary literary teapots are here: Are letters more noble than the profession of arms? Is rhyme necessary to poetry? Was Lucan a poet? When Pinciano makes the familiar point that Lucan was not a poet because his histories were not in verse, "Fadrique y Vgo se sonrieron," indulgent and weary smiles more possible around 1600 than earlier.

Of the thirteen *epístolas* directed to Pinciano's friend Don Gabriel, the least expected is the first one ("Introductión a la Philosophía antigua"), a synopsis of Aristotelian philosophy drawn from *On the Soul*, the *Nichomachean Ethics*, and other treatises, subject matter considerably removed from the literary considerations of the rest of Pinciano's book. Toward the end of this recorded conversation Pinciano sets down various definitions of beauty and draws upon Plato's *Phaedrus, Hippias*, and apparently the *Symposium*. The second epistle ("Prólogo de la Philosophía antigua") takes up the question of Plato as a *misómousos*, with attendant considerations on the ethical and social values of poetry. The third dialogue concerns the "essences and causes" of poetry; it treats of inspiration and the conflict of art and nature in the formation of a poet, a question on which Pinciano takes the middle position familiar to the humanists. The fourth epistle introduces the four major divisions of poetry: epic, comic, tragic, and dithyrambic, all of which will receive an individual chapter later. The fifth deals with *fábula* or plot structure and leans heavily on Aristotle for its explanations of unity, anagnorisis, verisimilitude, pity, and fear. Like Minturno, Pinciano views the function of tragedy as moving us to pity, fear, and wonder; this latter phenomenon of perturbation and admiration (τὸ θαυμαστόν of Aristotle) interests Pinciano and he divides it into three classes.

The sixth epistle occupies itself with rhetoric, style, and metaphor, bearing echoes of Aristotle and Cicero. The seventh epistle is devoted to meter and is perhaps the most conventional. Yet it was by no means the least important to Pinciano, who felt that before him there had existed no satisfactory poetic art or treatise on versification: "Assí que no condeno yo las métricas artes que hasta agora están escriptas, sino . . . a mí no satisfazen" (II, 218). The eighth letter discusses tragedy and its properties (*diferencias*) and parts. The only major deviation from Aristotle here is the development of *ethe* as meaning *costumbres*, as *ethos* was translated in Renaissance Greek lexicons. The ninth dialogue reconstructs an Aristotelian definition of comedy, an enterprise undertaken in more recent times by Lane Cooper. It is in this lesson that Pinciano claims *lo feo* and *lo torpe* to be the two underlying motivations of laughter, and records a welter of contemporary anecdotes, some Rabelaisian, and pigeonholes them into types of humor. Epistle X is devoted to the dithyrambic or *zarabanda*, which Pinciano insistently and apparently alone in the Renaissance considers one of the four major poetic genres, parallel to comic, tragic, and epic. The following dialogue ("De la Heroyca") contains two notable exegeses on the Homeric and Vergilian epics. In a fruitless effort to counteract the advice of Vives and forestall the Hojedas and the Valdivielsos, Pinciano cautions against writing Christian epics. He takes this occasion to remind the reader that his own national epic, *El Pelayo,* will be coming along shortly (III, 169, 298). Epistle XII returns to the minor poetic genres: satire, mime, eclogue, elegy, apologue, and epigram. The final dialogue echoes Scaliger's section, *Theatrum,* and treats of the art of "executing" or acting, the entire conversation transpiring within the walls of the theater where the trio is witnessing *Iphigenia.*

There is brilliance and subtlety in Pinciano's thinking. With a facile discussion (II, 361-62) he anticipates Croce's affirmation in the *Estetica* that the poet who is insincere and inconstant would betray his art if he did not appear insincere and inconstant in his writings. He is more aware than Aristotle that the operation of katharsis depends on the varying sensitivity of the onlookers to compassion and fear. He is apparently a minority of one in warning against the dangers of using verisimilitude as a criterion of judgment (II, 80).

Yet with Pinciano's learning and imagination there remains a strain of common sense which one associates with the Spanish realistic temperament, the Sancho mentality which raises practical objections. Aware of all the neo-Platonic, Plotinian, and Pythagorean digressions on the nature and definition of beauty of his century, he dismisses the question: "La hermosura de Platón . . . se estiende a mucho más que la nuestra; porque en Castilla solamente se dize hermoso el hombre o la mujer que tiene el semblante bien proporcionado" (I, 98-99). He is exceptionally clear-headed when it comes to the chivalric romances, especially if one remembers Tasso's tortuous attempts in his discourse on the heroic poem to fit them into the neo-Aristotelian definitions of epic with a Procrustean accommodation. Heroic and epic poems are worthy of Homer and Vergil (he does not hold one to be superior to the other, as did Scaliger); but clearly the very popular "libros de cauallerías" or romances are like the "fábulas milesias" of old and "carecen de fundamento verdadero" (II, 165; III, 154). This was certainly Sancho's own attitude about the romances on Amadís, Roland, and Palmerín. In a period when the humanists were still trying to judge vernacular poetry by classic prosody and create such anomalies as "vers baïfins," Pinciano declares in his discussion of the *arte mayor:* "que los castellanos no conocemos [sylabas] largas ni breves para el metro, ni aun creo que las pronunciamos con distinción" (II, 227-28).

Pinciano was a great summarizer and conciliator. Unbounded was his admiration for Aristotle, "que a los passados enseñó, y a los presentes y venideros amaestró" (I, 302). If it is true, as Spingarn states, that after 1536 Aristotle's authority as a natural philosopher declined as his literary authority increased, Pinciano pays homage to both sides of "the master of those who know." He ranks Aristotle as poet even higher than Pindar (III, 125). Yet "su maestro Platón" and Horace are synthesized with Aristotle in that "fusion" of which Marvin Herrick and Irene Samuels have written. Plato, too, becomes a substantive meaning "final authority": "Fadrique, cuyo paracer me es Platón" (II, 213). Whereas Pinciano complains that Horace is too brief and disorganized (I, 9), he is thoroughly steeped in the pithy precepts of Horace, as were all his contemporaries.

Although Pinciano habitually draws upon Greek or Latin authors to illustrate his points, remaining disappointingly parsimonious in his remarks on his compatriots, many perceptions of Siglo de Oro thinking are afforded by this treatise. That the lexical decorum characteristic of the later French classical theater was also observed in Spain is evidenced by the injunction against using even such a word as "jarro" on the stage (11, 195). A subtle condemnation of money as a factor of nobility comes out three decades before the social satire of the *Sueños* of Quevedo (I, 129). Since so much of Renaissance literary theory was expressed in an Italian, French, or English context, it is pleasing to find the familiar neo-Aristotelian covenants reappearing in a Spanish frame of reference— to learn that "meter is swallowed up by the *fábula,* as the Duero swallows up the Pisuerga at the bridge of Simancas" (I, 270). The very sententious quality of the spoken *réplicas* appeals to the student of proverbs, and much of the homespun, aphoristic wisdom which slips through the humanistic theory could well have come from the pages of Renaissance emblem books, a genre Pinciano remembers to discuss.

The greatest contemporary influence upon Pinciano was Julius

Caesar Scaliger. He praised Scaliger over Horace and Vida as a splendid teacher for young poets and urged his readers to read the Italo-French pedant (I, 10). Pinciano's catalogue of genres and literary forms follows in general the listing in Scaliger's first book. The *rapprochements* between the *Poetices libri septem* of Scaliger and the *Philosophía antigua poética* are too numerous to be developed here, but we offer a momentary sampling. When the *Philosophía* classifies Roman comedy as *pretextata, trabeata, tabernaria,* and *atelana,* it is translating in order Scaliger's *praetextata, trabeata, tabernaria,* and *atellana.* In Pinciano's discussion of whence authors take the titles of their works (III, 253), he follows Scaliger closely:

de la persona que se celebra, como la Eneyda de Eneas (III, 253)	del tiempo, como los Fastos (254)
A persona, Vlyssea, Aeneis, etc. (*Poetices, cxxiii*)	a tempore, quemadmodum de Fastis dicebamus. (ibid.)

In fact, Pinciano imitated Scaliger's bent for classifying so conscientiously that he leans back on an older tradition and subdivides prologues into four types where Scaliger had been content with one (III, 80). And whereas his contemporaries recognized two types of obscurity, intentional and unintentional, Pinciano adds a third type (II, 161) which is apparently about to be identified with *culteranismo.*

It is paradoxical that Pinciano's analytical dragnet does not come up with a discussion of one of the most characteristic genres of the Renaissance: the dialogue. To what extent the writers of the humanistic period felt that the dialogue must transcribe actual conversations and to what extent they may be fiction no Renaissance theorist has ever told us. As for himself, Pinciano claims to be a faithful recorder: "Pinciano se fué a la posada y trasladó lo oydo" (I, 301). Influenced by the Platonic dialogues, of whose authenticity they were uncertain, the Quattro- and Cinquecento writers sensed a creative license. Ugo asks, incidentally, "Pregunto: ¿los Diálogos y Coloquois en que Platón escriuió su doctrina passaron assí como él los dexó escritos? Sí o no. Claro está que pudiera acontescer, mas no acontescieron, de manera que imitó a lo que pudiera ser y no fué" (I, 200-1). This passage no doubt sheds light on the actual historicity of Pinciano's own trialogue.

These reprint editions of the Consejo aim at making available accurate texts rather than critical or annotated editions. Annotated editions of Pinciano and Luzán are still in order. Certain references to contemporaries remain unclarified (I, 214; I, 301).

It would be interesting to learn the sources of the many examples of humor used as illustrative materials. One such source is Lope de Rueda's *Aceitunas* (III, 45), which is identified only in the index. However, such editing would have delayed the appearance of this text for several years, and it was important for this erudite work to be more readily available than the edition of Muñoz Peña (as should the text of Luzán, available easily only in fragments in Cano's study). The scholarly world will thus be reminded that one or two poetic arts were produced in Spain which rival in completeness and subtlety and adherence to the neo-classic canons those of Scaliger and Castelvetro. That Pinciano leans occasionally on Scaliger is unimportant. Du Bellay plagiarized wholeheartedly from Sperone Speroni to write the most important poetic treatise of the French Renaissance. Pinciano is even superior to Scaliger and the Italians in his independence of expression and his enlarged views of the materials and substance of literary criticism, extending even to such items as theatrical costuming. Pinciano's considerable influence on Cervantes himself has been assessed by William C. Atkinson in "Cervantes, El Pinciano, and the *Novelas ejemplares*" (*Hispanic Review*, July, 1948) and by Sanford Shepard in a thesis on "López Pinciano and Aristotelian Literary Criticism in the Spanish Renaissance" (New York University, 1959), which demonstrates that Cervantes accepted Pinciano's transfer of epic theory to the novel and views this as the most significant result of the saturation of the Siglo de Oro by Aristotelian criticism. Pinciano's independence of expression is patently Spanish, but so also may be the extension of the frontiers of criticism. One cannot help remembering that Menéndez y Pelayo intended to include in the final volume of his history of criticism and aesthetics "la danza, la esgrima y la tauromaquia."

VI

THE AUTHENTICITY OF DE HOLLANDA'S
DIALOGOS EM ROMA

FRANCISCO DE HOLLANDA has been assured a modest paragraph in the ledger of history for three principal merits: he was a competent miniaturist, he was one of Portugal's most enthusiastic humanists, and he was a friend of Michelangelo Buonarroti. It was this friendship which constituted his chief claim to fame. In the month of October, 1538, Francisco was present at three conversations on art and aesthetics in which participated, among others, Michelangelo and his good friend Vittoria Colonna. Francisco recorded these conversations for posterity. Together with a fourth dialogue in which Michelangelo does not figure, these *Dialogos em Roma* form the latter half of Francisco's *Da pintura antigua,* published at Lisbon in 1548.

None can dispute the interest of these dialogues, but some scholars have disputed their authenticity. Arturo Farinelli, in his *saggio* on Dante and Michelangelo, calls them "alquanto fantistici."[1] Hans Tietze and Carlo Aru are disposed to reject the good faith of Francisco, considering them an arbitrary exercise in the dialogue *genre,* so popular in Renaissance Italy.[2] Other

1. A. Farinelli, *Michelangelo e Dante* (Turin, 1918), p. 40.
2. Hans Tietze, "Francisco de Hollanda und Donato Giannottis Dialoge und Michelangelo" in *Repertorium für Kunstwissenschaft,* XXVIII (1905), 295-320; Carlo Aru, "I dialoghi romani di Francisco de Hollanda" in *L'Arte,* XXI (1928), 117-28.

Although the contents of the present essay will serve as a refutation to most of the doubts of Tietze and Aru, certain immediate answers may be made here to several of their main points. Tietze admits more readily than Aru that the spirit of Michelangelo fills these dialogues. But both feel that De Hollanda consciously introduced Michelangelo into the dialogues so that the latter's remarks on patronage would win better treatment for art and artists in Spain and Portugal. Yet, however dictated by self-interest the composition of the *Dialogos* may have been, this does not necessarily disprove the accuracy of the report. In questioning why Michelangelo would dwell two times upon the patronage system in the Iberian Peninsula, Tietze and Aru disregard the fact that two members of this small company (Francisco de Hollanda and Vittoria Colonna's friend Diego Zapata) were from that area. Furthermore, Vittoria and her husband, the Marchese di Pescara, were interested in Spain, the latter irritating his countrymen considerably by declaring that he would rather have been born in Spain than in Italy.

Both Tietze and Aru object to certain statements attributed to Michelangelo by De Hollanda on the grounds that they resemble in a general way opinions

authorities, such as Elías Tormo, are more credulous: "Después de leer el libro no habrá quien dude de la autenticidad de los coloquios tenidos en San Silvestre!"[3] Indeed many scholars have sided with Tormo (*vide infra*, note 63.)

To the present writer the *Dialogos em Roma* seem authentic in both letter and spirit. If one reads them immediately upon setting down the collected letters and *Rime* of Michelangelo, they ring surprisingly true. In attempting to demonstrate their authenticity as reliably as one can after four centuries, we have two paths of investigation open to us—exterior evidence and inner evidence.

When one is dealing with a historical figure about whom so few biographical facts are known, a demonstration of authenticity based on exterior evidence becomes an ingenious but unreliable exercise in detectivism. There are a few data adduced by the historians which might help us conclude that the *Dialogos* are genuine. The mere fact that Francisco was a friend of Buonarroti is attested by a cordial personal letter sent from Lisbon to Rome, August 15, 1553.[4] It is historically proved that Michelangelo visited Vittoria Colonna frequently in the garden of the Church of San Silvestro. One of her invitations to him still exists: "Se voi non sete oggi in lavoro, potressi venire a parlarmi con vostra comodità."[5] One can add these facts to other historical evidence and demonstrate with reasonable certainty that Francisco de Hollanda did actually meet with Michelangelo, Vittoria Colonna, Lattanzio Tolomei, Fra Ambrosio da Siena, and others, much as he described it. But all these data together still cannot prove the veracity of the dialogues as recorded. In fact, no exterior evidence

---

found in other Renaissance treatises on art (by Alberti, Leonardo, *et al.*) Most of Aru's article is predicated on this objection, and this is its major weakness. In no way does he ever prove or try to prove that De Hollanda would be more likely to know or draw upon these sources than would Michelangelo. As a speaker in the *Dialogos*, Michelangelo very possibly echoed certain ideas on art which he had gathered from his contemporaries; this in no way invalidates the *Dialogos* as an authentic document. Furthermore, Michelangelo's poems and letters often present a closer correlation with his quoted statements than is offered by the contemporary treatises on art, as we hope to demonstrate in these pages.

3. Francisco de Hollanda, *De la pintura antigua*, ed. by E. Tormo (Madrid, 1921), p. xxiv.

4. Quoted in Francisco de Hollanda, *Da pintura antigua*, ed. by J. de Vasconcellos (Porto, 1930), pp. 337-38.

5. *Carteggio di Vittoria Colonna* (Turin, 1892), p. 207.

could of itself establish at this late date whether Francisco recorded honestly what he heard.

Can examination of the internal evidence prove more fruitful? We believe that it remains the only way to make an honest appraisal of Francisco's veracity. By inner evidence we understand the words themselves which he attributed to Michelangelo and to the others. By studying and systematizing the principal statements of Michelangelo recorded in the *Dialogos,* we shall endeavor to show that they coincide with and complement opinions which he voiced in his letters and poetry. We shall note how accurately De Hollanda captured the attitudes and personality of Michelangelo as we know them through other sources. In a few instances our attempt to demonstrate the truthfulness of Francisco will lean on testimony of such contemporaries as Condivi and Vasari.

In this enterprise we shall not choose a few hand-picked passages which tend to support our view, but shall select the dominant themes or opinions which constitute the bulk of Michelangelo's remarks. These passages will fall under the following headings: inspiration and genius, religious motivation of art, differentiation of the arts, exclusiveness (Ivory-Towerism) of the artist, the financial rewards of art, social value of art, nationalistic ideas, personal characteristics, and biographical data.

Whereas most of the aestheticians and literary theorists of the Renaissance adhered to the usual classical vocabulary in ascribing genius to an artist or poet, Michelangelo relied upon one particular word to describe genius. The term was *intelletto. Intelletto* was a sort of divine insight granted sparingly to an elect and granted at or before birth. This key word for genius, which we shall find in Michelangelo's poems treating of art, is specifically attributed to Michelangelo at least three times in the *Dialogos em Roma.* While the other collocutors employ various words to denote genius (*engenho, spirito, graça, entendimento,* etc.) Buonarroti uses the conspicuous word *inteleito* in a most characteristic manner in De Hollanda's chronicle.

At one point Michelangelo notes that a great painter eschews conversation with those incompetent in the fine arts lest the latter should profane his genius (*abaxarem o inteleito*).[6] Later Michel-

6. Vasconcellos edition (see note 4), p. 185. All quotations from the *Dialogos* will refer to pagination of this edition [D] hereafter. All references to Michelangelo's poetry will apply to the *Rime* [R] (Florence, Rinascimento del libro, 1927), edited by Papini. Letters are quoted from *Lettere di Michelangelo Buonarroti* [L] (Lanciano, 1910), 2 vols., edited by Papini.

angelo informs Messer Lattanzio that a successful painter should lead a saintly life "para no seu *inteleito* poder inspirar o *Sprito Sancto*."[7] Or again, he posits that paintings are copies of the perfect creations of God and, like music, something only the *inteleito* can sense.[8]

The difference between the competent painters and the inept depends precisely upon this innate feeling for beauty:

Mas nunca soube desejar bem nesta sciencia senão aquele entendimento que entende o bem e quanto pode alançar d'elle. E esta é grave cousa do stremo e deferença que ha entre o desejo do alto entendimento na pintura ao baxo.[9]

Whether or not De Hollanda here translated Michelangelo's *intelletto* as *entendimento*, the thought is typical of Michelangelo.

Equally authentic appear those passages where Francisco records Michelangelo's definition of a painter as one who merely finds beauties in nature. There is Michelangelo's reference to the painter as "habil para inventar o que inda não é achado."[10] There is his quotation about God telling Moses that He will bestow upon good painters the genius to invent (*i.e.* find) beauties: "dizendo Deos a Mouses que elle lhes enfunderia sapiencia e inteligencia do seu sprito para poderem inventar e fazer tudo quanto fazer e inventar podesse."[11]

It is easy to find proof in Michelangelo's written works that this concept and even the specific word *intelletto* occupied a crucial place in his aesthetics. The theory that the artist merely discovers art forms which have existed before him and will survive him is the theme of Michelangelo's stanza "Si come per levar, Donna, si pone" and his madrigal "Negli anni molti e nelle molte pruove."[12] In each piece Michelangelo mentions nature's sealing artistic forms "in pietra alpestra e dura." The most famous quatrain in which he uses the word *intelletto* to take his Platonic view of art is contained in his sonnet LXXXIII beginning:

> Non ha l'ottimo artista alcun concetto
> C' un marmo solo in sè non circoscriva
> Col suo soverchio: e solo a quello arriva
> La mano che ubbidisce all'intelletto.[13]

7. *D*, p. 235.
8. *D*, p. 190.
9. *D*, p. 234.
10. *D*, pp. 208-9.
11. *D*, p. 236.
12. *R*, pp. 81, 129.
13. *R*, p. 81.

In fact, Michelangelo even affirms that harmonies preexist in the ink of the writer as in the marble of the sculptor.[14]

Thus Michelangelo's theories on genius and the role of the artist, curiously compounded of Christian, Platonic, and perhaps even Provençal elements, are faithfully recorded in the *Dialogos em Roma*. It seems scarcely possible that these passages were invented out of whole cloth.

The same may be said for those passages treating of Michelangelo's very Christian notions on artistic inspiration. Michelangelo was one of the most devout men of the Renaissance, lay or clergy. His religiosity definitely affected his aesthetic thinking. Thus he affirmed of painting, "Esta nobelissima sciencia não é de nenhuma terra, que do ceo veio."[15] In the third dialogue Messer Lattanzio presses Michelangelo for a definition of painting, and the latter immediately obliges. His is a definition which only a deeply religious man could have formulated:

Sómente a pintura, que eu tanto celebro e louvo, será emitar alguma só cousa das que o imortal Deos fez, com grande cuidado e sapiencia, e que elle inventou e pintou, semelhantes ao mestre, e d'aqui para baxo, seja, ou as alimarias e as aves, despensando a perfeção, segundo o merece cada cousa. E por sentença minha, aquella é a excellente e divina pintura que mais se parece e melhor emita qualquer obra do imortal Deos. . . .[16]

Since lofty painting is "only a copy of the perfections of God and an echo of His own painting," it is destined to inspire devotion in the onlooker. In the first dialogue Michelangelo says:

E a boa [pintura] d'esta não ha cousa mais nobre nem devota, porque a devoção, nos discretos nenhuma cousa a faz mais lembrar nem erguer que a deficuldade da perfeição que se vai unir e ajuntar a Deos.[17]

In a later dialogue Michelangelo discusses specifically the sacred task of painting the face of God, Christ, or the Virgin. He states that the artist must provoke contemplation, tears, reverence, and fear, and notes regretfully that "muitas vezes as imagens mal pintadas distraem e fazem perder a devoção, ao menos aos que tem pouca."[18] Elsewhere in this third dialogue the query arises: Is it better to paint quickly or leisurely? Michelangelo ventures a typical opinion:

14. *R*, p. 52.
15. *D*, p. 191.
16. *D*, p. 239.
17. *D*, pp. 189-90.
18. *D*, p. 236.

Eu vos direi: fazer com grande ligereiza e destreza qualquer cousa é muito proveitoso e bom; e dom é recebido do imortal Deos que aquilo que outro stá pintando em muitos dias, se faça em poucas horas.[19]

Michelangelo's firm belief in divine inspiration, amply recorded by De Hollanda, was an integral part of his aesthetics. It coincides with ideas expressed in several of his poems and letters. Aru's claim that these views of Michelangelo on divinity of inspiration derived from some comparable remarks of Alberti's would seem to indicate a misunderstanding of Michelangelo's basic theory of art.[20] Confirming Buonarroti's recorded remark, "a pintura do ceo veio," is his reference to his work, in a letter to Niccolò Martelli, as "quell'arte che Dio m'a data."[21] Of the other poems dealing with the divine inspiration of art,[22] one characterizes God as the original and supreme artist: "Colui che 'l tutto fe' colla sua divin' arte."[23] Another is especially worthy of partial reproduction:

> Se il mio rozzo martello i duri sassi
>   Forma d'uman aspetto or questo or quello,
>   Dal ministro, che 'l guida iscorge e tiello,
>   Prendendo il moto va con gli altrui passi.
> Ma quel divino, che in cielo alberga e stassi,
>   Altri, e sè più, col proprio andar fa bello.[24]

Both Michelangelo's letters and the dialogues contain discussions turning upon comparison and differentiation of the arts. From the letters one notes a gradual evolution in Michelangelo's ideas. In order to establish the veracity of his purported remarks in 1538, the year of the dialogues, one must prove that these remarks coincide with opinions expressed in letters from this same period, although they may differ from Michelangelo's opinions written earlier and later in his life. Such a proof is entirely possible.

In the second dialogue Francisco states without being contradicted that Michelangelo is a painter and not primarily a sculptor: "o grande debuxador M. Angelo, que aqui stá, sculpe tambem em marmor, que não é seu officio."[25] He adds that Michelangelo

19. *D*, p. 241.
20. Aru, *op. cit.*, p. 122.
21. *L*, I, 155.
22. *R*, pp. 126, 139.
23. *R*, p. 3.
24. *R*, p. 93.
25. *D*, p. 206.

himself now feels sculpture a less challenging and demanding art than painting. The Florentine, without gainsaying Francisco, takes the floor with a long apologia for painting as the most universal art and the one most immediately identified with design:

Comoquer que tanto me ponho ás vezes a cuidar e a imaginar que acho entre os homens não haver mais que uma só arte ou sciencia e esta ser o debuxar ou pintar, de que tudo o al são membros que procedem.[26]

This higher esteem for painting than for sculpture, which may surprise at first and which Aru found scarcely credible, is not out of character.

True, in Michelangelo's earlier years the "prime art" was sculpture, with architecture second. Almost all his letters after he first went to Rome were signed "Michelagniolo scultore"—until 1526, in fact[27]—and he advised his family to address their communications to "Michelagniolo Buonarroti scultor in Roma." The period during which he did the paintings of the Sistine Chapel (1508-12) marked his most insistent claims that he was not a painter. It is common knowledge that, when commissioned for the Sistine ceiling, he declared painting was not his art, that the appointment was being made by Bramante so that the latter's nephew Raphael would benefit by the contrast. When this painting got off to a poor start, he complained to the Pope: "Lo avevo pur detto a Vostra Santità che io non ero pittore."[28] At the close of a poem telling of his vexations in producing the world's most historic painting he adds the disclaimer, "nè io pittore."[29] By April, 1543, he was urging his family to discard the title of sculptor when writing him.[30] In fact, by 1542, four years after the dialogues in San Silvestro, he was signing letters "pittor in Roma" and even claims about Raphael, "ciò che aveva dell'arte l'aveva da me." It is apparent that in October, 1538, when Lattanzio Tolomei admitted Francisco into the inner circle on Monte Cavallo, Michelangelo's ideas on the relative importance of painting had evolved to the stage one notes in his letters composed shortly thereafter. By 1542 he was boasting of his painting and by 1546 promised a painting for Francis I of France.

Further evidence of the authenticity of the *Dialogos* must

26. *D*, p. 207.

27. *L*, i, 137. Aru (p. 126) intimates that the terminal date is only 1512, apparently forgetting these later letters to Fattucci and Spina.

28. H. Grimm, *Michelangelo* (Milan, 1875), pp. 280-81.

29. *R*, p. 7.

30. *L*, ii, 16.

be added here. In the third colloquy Michelangelo admits a tendency to abolish distinctions among the arts. As design (*desenho* or *debuxo*) is the common denominator of all arts, one must question the existence of real distinctions between painting, sculpture, and architecture.[31] In fact, an artist who has acquired a sense of design ought to be competent in all these arts. Evidence of this conclusion is present in Michelangelo's letter to his friend, the historian Varchi. Here he claims that there should be no dispute about relative values of the arts. Both painting and sculpture serve the same purpose, he agrees, and arise from the same experience and inspiration.[32] Michelangelo's insistence upon design and draftsmanship as fundamentals of art breaks out in his emphatic note on an Antonio Mini copy of one of his drawings: "Disegnia Antonio, disegnia Antonio, disegnia, non perder tempo."

Michelangelo's doctrinary feelings about genius created a definite cleavage between the chosen few and the incompetent or indiscriminate many. In his works he placed emphasis upon classic sublimity and developed a Horatian scorn for those without *intelletti* who could not fully appreciate his conceptions. This attitude is apparent in several passages of the *Dialogos em Roma*. In the third causerie he rails against the *profanum vulgus.*

Mas comoquer que o vulgo da gente sem juizo ama sempre o que devia de avorrecer, e aquillo vitupera que merece mais louvor, não é muito de spantar de errar tão constantemente acerca da pintura, arte não dina senão de altos entendimentos.[33]

In an earlier dialogue Michelangelo conjures a picture of a solitary man of genius pestered by the idle and uncritical.[34] He questions why idle people, of whom the artist asks nothing, should expect so much from him. "Não sabeis que ha hi sciencias que querem todo o homem, sem deixarem d'elle nada desocupado ás vossas ociosidades?" In this same passage he bluntly states that artists corrupt their genius in such useless talk. The best proof of the authenticity of this sentiment is the manner in which Michelangelo based his conduct upon it. Not only does one read in the letters (*passim*) that Buonarroti prefers to lead a sequestered life, but there are at least two contemporary witnesses as well, Condivi and Vasari. These two biographers take pains to

31. *D*, p. 238.
32. *L*, II, 79-80.
33. *D*, p. 234.
34. *D*, p. 186.

explain that Michelangelo's preference for solitude is not the result of pride (Condivi) or eccentricity (Vasari).[35] Other passages of the *Dialogos em Roma* express a scorn for the vulgar throng, not excluding wealthy art patrons themselves.[36]

Even in Buonarroti's poetry one reads that good taste is rare and that the world perforce is blind. Among the stanzas to Tommaso Cavalieri one reads:

> Il buon gusto è si raro
> C' al vulgo errante cede
> In vista, allor che dentro di sè gode. . .
> Il mondo è cieco.[37]

He also deprecates the *vulgo cieco* in the sonnet "La nuova alta beltà ch' in ciel terrei." And certainly Michelangelo must have cried "Il mondo è cieco" when he heard of the plans to place vivid drapery on the figures of his *Giudizio universale*.

A verification of the *Dialogos em Roma* turns up in an unexpected quarter, in the *Ragionamento del Gello sopra le difficoltà di mettere in regola la lingua che si parla in Firenze* (1551). In the *Dialogos* Michelangelo decrees that an artistic creation should appear the product of effortless nature rather than of studied art, that it should appear "depois de mui trabalhada, que foi feita quasi depressa e quasi sem nenhum trabalho, e muito levemente, não sendo assi."[38] In Gellius one reads, "Michelangelo was wont to say that only those figures were good from which one had removed the effortful labor, that is, produced with such skill that they appeared the result of nature rather than art."[39] Gellius could not have copied this statement from De Hollanda, nor does it seem plausible that De Hollanda could have borrowed it from him.

Penury and financial dependency constituted a veritable calvary for Michelangelo. Although he claimed in his letters to come from an aristocratic *stirpe*, his was certainly an impoverished family. Financial concern colored his very patterns of thinking and action, as the letters abundantly testify. There is no mention of finances in the poetry, but those who knew Buonarroti through letters or conversation must have been struck by this preoccupa-

35. Quoted in Francisco de Hollanda, *Quatre dialogues sur la peinture*, ed. by L. Rouanet (Paris, 1911), p. xxviii.

36. *D*, pp. 228, 230, etc.

37. *R*, p. 130.

38. *D*, p. 242.

39. Quoted in 1746 edition of Condivi, p. 75.

tion. In any case, the long succession of references to money in the *Dialogos* convince at least this reader that Michelangelo was being faithfully quoted. In characteristic fashion he rails against patrons who will not pay the artist a living wage, finding the Spanish grandees particularly reprehensible.[40] He complains that patrons who hold the purse strings know naught of art, often reward incompetent painters well while remaining stingy toward worthy artists.[41] He recalls with a touch of envy those painters of antiquity who destroyed their works rather than accept a niggardly fee for them.[42] He complains that in peacetime princes waste money on futile things while artists go unrewarded.[43]

Vittoria Colonna praises the generosity of Michelangelo with the qualifying remark, "e nisso sois eicelente, porque vós daes emfim como discreto liberal, e não como prodigo inorante."[44] This is precisely the impression one gathers *passim* from the *Lettere*, which prove Buonarroti generous to others, especially members of his family, but demanding concessions in return and specifying how the bounty should best be used.

Michelangelo's rancorous attitude toward patrons, continually articulated in the dialogues, is expressed throughout his correspondence. His very first letters from Rome tell that he cannot collect his wages and expense account to start drafting the work in the Sistine Chapel. They report how he was thrown bodily from the room when he tried to collect expenses from Pope Julius.[45] Other letters picture him fleeing penniless from creditors, losing his belongings to meet his taxes, and combatting poverty.[46] In 1560 he writes that he has labored seventeen years *gratis* in the fabric of St. Peter's.[47] There are many more passages describing resentment of his patrons. The writer of these letters and the speaker of the *Dialogos em Roma* seem indeed one and the same.

Condivi may be called upon again to support the veracity of our Francisco. Much of the third dialogue is occupied by an account of Michelangelo's role in the defense of Florence in 1529. He was one of those entrusted with the fortifications when the

40. *D*, p. 227.
41. *D*, p. 228.
42. *D*, p. 230.
43. *D*, p. 225.
44. *D*, p. 184.
45. *L*, ii, 12.
46. *L*, ii, 30.
47. *L*, ii, 149.

Spaniards besieged the town. Michelangelo makes rather surprising claims for his art when he explains how painting enabled him to devise machines of war and buttress city walls against enemy projectiles by means of wool-filled sandbags.[48] Condivi's description of Buonarroti's activities in organizing defensive measures agrees with the artist's own testimony in the *Dialogos*, even to a reference to the wool-filled "mattresses."[49] As Condivi's biography of Michelangelo appeared in July, 1553, De Hollanda could not have utilized it. Michelangelo's account in the *Dialogos* is further substantiated by Vasari, following Condivi, by the artist's friend Giannotti in his *Della repubblica fiorentina*, and by Busini's *Lettere sopra l'assedio di Firenze* (addressed to Varchi and not especially favorable to Buonarroti).

The Renaissance conception of Italy as the home of the third classicism (Hellas ➡ Rome ➡ Italy) was obviously shared by Michelangelo. According to De Hollanda, he felt sincerely that little art created outside the peninsula (even by Albrecht Dürer) was of first-rate quality.[50] Of Italy he opines, "Nella se fazem as obras da pintura illustre mais mestriosas e gravemente que em nenhuma outra parte," and "chamamos á boa pintura italiana."[51] In the third dialogue these feelings crystallize into advice to Francisco never to leave Italy, lest he regret it.[52] He shows his partiality toward the city of Rome itself when speaking of painting as "aquella virtude que sempre será stimada emquanto houver ahi homens em Italia e cidade."[53]

The authenticity of this prideful feeling for Italy is attested in Michelangelo's letters by his frequent praise of various Italian artists, whereas no praise is wasted upon foreigners. It is also attested by his unwillingness to leave Italy, although he was strongly urged to do so by foreign monarchs.[54] Even more numerous are letters proving his attachment for Rome. He constantly re-

48. *D*, p. 222.

49. Condivi, *Vita*, sec. xliii. Cf. further testimony in Giambattista Busini, *Lettere a Benedetto Varchi sopra l'assedio di Firenze* (Florence, 1861), pp. 103-15, and Donato Giannotti, *Della Repubblica fiorentina* (Venice, 1722), pp. 273-74.

50. Tietze (p. 307) expresses surprise that Michelangelo should condemn Flemish painting so volubly, but Aru admits that the recorded condemnation corresponds with Michelangelo's known feelings.

51. *D*, pp. 190-91.

52. *D*, pp. 228, 229.

53. *D*, p. 228.

54. Among these were Francis I, Emperor Charles V, and Bayezid the Turk.

fuses commissions which would take him away from the capital. He orders his relatives to buy a house in Florence where he may spend his last years; but Michelangelo never could make up his mind to leave Rome, and there he died at a ripe old age.

De Hollanda mentions several personal characteristics and offhand remarks of Michelangelo which sound quite lifelike. Buonarroti's allusion to his diminished physical forces[55] sounds typical of a man who claims that for every day he works he must spend four days resting, or the man who admits losing twenty pounds working for the Pope.[56] Michelangelo's somber character is illustrated by Francisco's chance remark, "Riu-se, sem a senhora Marquesa, outra vez." ("He laughed again, despite the absence of Vittoria Colonna.")[57] A reading of Michelangelo's letters leaves one with the impression that he was a man who seldom laughed, and that only his closest friends saw him smile.[58] Vittoria Colonna would be one of these. Vittoria herself alludes in the *Dialogos* to his short temper. She wonders whether Michelangelo "agora não usará algum stremo, dos que com outrem costuma?"[59] In the letters Buonarroti tends to lose his patience rather easily, especially with popes and with members of his family.[60] The irony of Michelangelo is not absent from the *Dialogos em Roma*. When De Hollanda states that Portuguese noblemen neither understand nor esteem painting, Michelangelo comments laconically, "Fazem bem!"[61] The chroniclers have recorded several examples of this irony,[62] lending further evidence that the dialogues capture not only Buonarroti's thoughts and persuasions, but also his characteristics.

As the meager exterior evidence brought to light by such competent scholars as Vasconcellos and Raczynski will never enable us to decide with certainty the truthfulness or mendacity

55. *D*, p. 217.
56. *L*, i, 147.
57. *D*, p. 227.
58. Cf. Auguste Barbier, *Jambes et poèmes* (Paris, 1888), p. 127: "Comme Dante, on dirait que tu n'as jamais ri."
59. *D*, p. 188.
60. See especially Letter xlv, *postscriptum.*
61. *D*, p. 194.
62. There is his scoffing comment that the dome of the Florentine cathedral resembled a bird cage. Or his rejoinder when told that Vasari's paintings of the life of Paul III had been executed in only 100 days: "E' si conosce!" Yet another instance may be drawn from the dialogues themselves—his observation that Flemish painting will please very young and very old women, as well as nuns and friars. *Cf.* also Condivi, *Vita*, sec. lxviii.

of De Hollanda, inner evidence as recorded above will probably remain as reliable a clue as we shall have. Had this essay presented a collection of random remarks of Michelangelo easily correlated with his letters and rimes, those remarks would scarcely have constituted conclusive evidence. However, it has aimed at bringing together passages sampling every major pronouncement of Buonarroti in the *Dialogos*. It thus affords a collective body of evidence which (substantiated by the opinions of the *Lettere*, the *Rime*, with Condivi, Vasari, Gellius, *et al.*—all sources De Hollanda could not have known) enables us to believe in the dialogues and, as they say in Portuguese, "stick" Francisco at his word.[63] In sum, one may criticize the portrait of Michelangelo in the dialogues only as one might criticize Francisco de Hollanda's single extant drawing of his idol Buonarroti: one might wish for more details, but the accuracy of what one has is attested by a comparison with other evidence.

63. The number of scholars who have accepted Francisco's truthfulness, and indeed made use of his testimony, exceeds that of the doubters. Symonds admits that "we may fairly accept his account of these famous conferences as a truthful transcript (*Michelangelo*, II, 116). Menéndez y Pelayo finds in De Hollanda's *reportages* "such spontaneous and simple diction with such honest enthusiasm that they exclude any notion of fiction or theoretical artifice, . . ." (*Historia de las ideas estéticas*, IV, 112.) Although discerning a certain "polemic accentuation" in them, Mariani uses them quite readily (*Michelangelo*, p. 218). Confronted with identical evidence in Vasari and De Hollanda, Buscaroli concludes, "The equivalence is such . . . that it could not be explained without supposing the information to be from the selfsame source, Michelangelo himself" (*Il concetto dell'arte nelle parole di Michelangelo*, p. 9). The most forthright claim is made for the *Dialogos* by Emilio Radius, for whom they "constitute as much as there remains of Michelangelo's aesthetics" (*Colloqui con Michelangelo*, p. 21).

Typical of the general Italian acceptance of De Hollanda are the specific defenses of Irene Cattaneo, *La Vie d'Italie*, March, 1928; A. M. Bessone Aurelij, "Della sincerità di Francisco d'Olanda," *Il Vasari* (1930), and Bianca Toscana, *Il pensiero di Michelangelo sull'arte* (Naples, 1951) p. 34.

Talking with a number of art historians in Lisbon on this matter in 1953, I found the tendency in Portugal was to accept De Hollanda as an utterly respectable humanist and reporter of the ideas of his time.

VII

MARGUERITE DE NAVARRE AND DANTE

THE QUESTION of the ascendancy of Dante over the thought of Marguerite d'Angoulême has interested students of the French Renaissance, for this lady has been generally recognized as the leading *italianisant* of her century. Several passages have been noted in her poetry which seem to be of Dantesque origin. But because the problem merits fuller attention than it has received to date,[1] and because the brief discussions of these passages appear to be as debatable as they are incomplete, a fuller examination is in order. Farinelli, Hauvette, Pellegrini, and Jourda affirm that Dante played a great part in the spiritual and literary formation of the Pearl of Princesses.[2] Others have adhered to this opinion, although merely repeating or translating the conclusions of these four scholars.[3] The only dissenting note is struck by M. Auguste Renaudet in his short review of Jourda's definitive life of Marguerite. For his part, he suspects the thesis first propounded by Farinelli to be ill-founded and ill-proved, and

---

1. In the *Revue des études italiennes* (avril-sept., 1936, p. 154) Giulio Bertoni indicates the need for further study of Marguerite's Italianism.

2. A. Farinelli, *Dante e la Francia*, I, 356: "Marguerite de Navarre aveva con magiche chiavi aperto il tempio in cui, solitario, non turbato da voci importune, Dante posava. Quand'ella usciva di vita, si chiuse il tempio, spariron le chiavi, e nessuno più, per molti anni, le ha ritrovate."

Carlo Pellegrini, *La prima opera di Margherita di Navarra* (Catania, 1920), p. 6: "Essa più e meglio assai ai Christine de Pisan aveva dimostrato di comprendere e di sentire in tutta la sua grandezza il poema dantesco." Professor Pellegrini's *Riflessi di cultura italiana nella prima opera di M. di N.* contains little new for our purposes.

H. Hauvette, *Etudes sur la Divine Comédie* (1922), p. 165. (Cf. also his article in the *Annales de l'université de Grenoble* [1899], t. XI.) ". . . la femme qui, dans son siècle, devait le mieux comprendre, lorsque, dans les dernières années de sa vie, attristée par des chagrins et des deuils de toutes sortes, elle trouva dans la lecture du divin poème une nourriture vraiment appropriée aux besoins de son cœur meurtri. Alors elle comprit toute la profondeur de la pensée de Dante."

Pierre Jourda, *Marguerite d'Angoulême* (Paris, 1930), I, 371: "Par le cœur, comme par la pensée, elle devait se sentir tout proche de Dante."

3. In her *Margherita di Navarra* (Turin, 1908), p. 219, C. Garosci, for example, paraphrases Farinelli: "Dante . . . che quasi solo nel suo secolo Margherita comprese subendone l'influenza spirituale."

briefly suggests that the Queen could never have penetrated the thought and the lesson of the *Commedia*.[4]

We know that Marguerite had access to three of Dante's works. There was a "libvre de Dante" in her father's library;[5] in addition to the *Commedia*, there was also a copy of the *Canzoni* at her next home, the château of Blois;[6] Fontainebleau and Paris, where so many of her middle years were spent, had copies of the epic;[7] there were also the manuscripts of Bergaigne and Minut.[8] Farinelli's statement that the *Convivio* was unknown to France in her lifetime and therefore inaccessible to the Queen is untrue; we have located a copy at Fontainebleau (see note 7). However, the mere presence of a volume need not imply a knowledge of its contents on the part of the Queen. Nor must the presence at court of the exegeses of Jacopo della Lana and Cristoforo Landino or of the commentaries of Luigi Alamanni lead us to conclude that she made use of them.

Marguerite mentions Dante not three[9] but four times in her entire works.[10] In order to establish those periods when she was supposedly engrossed in the *Commedia*, we shall attempt to record her mentions of Dante's name in chronological order. In addition, we shall try to evaluate and interpret these passages.

In 1534 Marguerite writes to King Francis I, her brother, a

4. A. Renaudet, *Revue du seizième siècle*, t. XVIII, 1931, p. 272.

5. E. Sénémand, *Bibliothèque de Charles d'Orléans, comte d'Angoulême, au château de Cognac en 1496* (Paris, 1861), p. 27.

6. H. Omont, *Anciens inventaires et catalogues de la Bibliothèque nationale* (*passim*).

7. I. Dorez, *Dante*, pp. 109 and 250; Jourda, *op. cit.*, I, 372. Several texts of Dante that Marguerite might have used we have noted in a catalogue of the Bibliothèque nationale, *Les manuscrits de Dante* (Paris, Thorin, 1892) on pages 25, 46, 65, 155: *p. 25:* Le MS 72 peut être identifié avec celui qui est ainsi décrit dans le catalogue de l'ancienne bibliothèque de Blois, de 1518: *Dante, l'Enfer, Purgatoire et Paradis*, couvert de veloux tanné; *p. 46:* Italien, MS 534, Fontainebleau: *L'Enfer*, avec traduction italienne du commentaire latin de Graziolo de' Bambaglioli; *p. 65:* Italien, MS 537, les gloses de Jacopo della Lana; *p. 155:* Italien, MS 1014 (ancien fonds 7768): Le *Convivio* de Dante, volume en parchemin. 138 feuillets. Ecriture de la fin du XVe siècle. Reliure en maroquin rouge, aux armes de France. The following note is appended: "Italien, le *Banquet* et *Convivo* de Dante florentin en prose a été tracé, au XVIe siècle, sur le verso au premier feuillet; ce volume figurait alors dans la collection de Fontainebleau."

8. P. Jourda, *op. cit.*, I, 372.

9. As Jourda states, *ibid.* I, 371.

10. These passages have not been collected by those very scholars who would make of Marguerite a student of Dante.

letter partially reproduced below,[11] which no commentator seems disposed to take seriously.[12] This first mention of Dante comes late, when Marguerite is in her forty-second year. Ten years have passed since the composition of the *Dialogue en forme de vision nocturne* (see below.) It is a bizarre idea of Dante that she presents in her letter. She sees in Dante a pitiful mortal possessed of libidinous passions which mature age should have checked, a Dante regretting days "qui ne se peuvent ratteindre"—apparently an allusion to the *nessun maggior dolore*. This conception of the Florentine she repeats elsewhere. The letter provides two sidelights on her knowledge of Dante. First, Dante remains for the Queen the poet of the first canti of the *Inferno*. Second, she compares this Dante with herself. At the time of his vision, Dante was thirty-five years of age; she makes him forty, approximately her own age. Furthermore, she identifies herself with him, as she does at the outset of several of her principal poems, and the letter becomes a document of paramount importance in the emotional life of the Queen.[13] Taken literally or not, this letter shows that Marguerite misinterpreted completely the serious motives for which Dante wrote the *Commedia*.

The second allusion to Dante is found in the LVth tale of the *Heptaméron*, published posthumously in 1559 and composed most probably between 1540 and 1548. The text of the LXVIth tale refers to events occurring in 1548; the LVth tale may therefore have been written about this time or shortly before. The mention of Dante is an incidental, detached paraphrase of the counsel "Non ragioniam di loro, ma guarda e passa," which Hircan rightfully attributes to Dante's Vergil. Marguerite borrows a phrase from the part of the *Commedia* that she knows; that is all.

11. Reproaching herself for an "ennuy pris" while reflecting on the happier days of the past, she complains:

> O! que je voy d'erreur la teste ceindre
> A ce Dante qui nous vient icy peindre
> Son triste enfer et vieille passion
>   D'ung ennuy pris.
> A quarante ans vouloir encores faindre
> D'avoir le mal que l'age doit refraindre.
> Puis par despit courre à devocion
> Prenant tan pour ferme ficsion
> C'est une fin plus qu' ensuivre à craindre
>   D'ung ennuy pris.

Nouvelles lettres de Marguerite d'Angoulême (Paris, 1841), pp. 122-23.

12. P. Pellegrini, *op. cit.*, p. 3; A. Farinelli, *op. cit.* 1, 331.

13. It is the source of Génin's charge of incest between her and Francis I.

The third direct allusion is found in the *Prisons* (*circa* 1545), the tripartite poem which, with the exception of the *Petit Oeuvre*, is most akin to Dante. Toward the end of the second "book," the Poet enumerates the three vices to which man is subjected. Admitting an inability to write *au vray* on the subject, he advises his mistress to read Dante and the canon of Saint John and of the three beasts symbolizing sins:

> C'est assavoir l'ourse, lyonne et louve[14]

and he adds:

> Je m'en tairay de peur d'estre reprins,
> Comme j'estoys lorsque je vous aprins
> Tout le discours de Dante et son histoire.

Marguerite interprets these animals as figures of *la chair, l'avarice,* and *l'orgueil de vie* respectively. Although this interpretation is at variance with the glosses of Della Lana, it coincides exactly with the *Dotta & leggiadra sposizione* of Cristoforo Landino, published at Venice in 1536. For once the Dantean allegory is fully understood.

The fourth mention—the verses reproduced by La Ferrière-Percy[15]—alludes once again to the *Inferno:*

> Douleur n'y a qu'au temps de la misère
> Se recorder de l'heureux et prospère,
> Comme autrefoys en Dante j'ay trouvé.

This time she finds some truth in the "triste enfer et vieille passion." But this borrowing of a tercet already become a commonplace indicates no ascendancy of thought or philosophy.

What do these four mentions tell of Marguerite's debt to the *Commedia?* From the letter of 1534 one concludes that she understood a human—*allzumenschlich*—Dante, a wayward sinner beset by allegorized sins, the principal of which was lust. The direct mention in the second book of the *Prisons* concerns this same sinful Dante. As for the *Livre de dépenses* and its translation of the *nessun maggior dolore,* one must remember that this passage of Dante was widely known in that century so extremely fond of

14. Lefranc's edition reads *l'ourse* for what is evidently *lonze.* Comte fails to make this rectification, but Farinelli and Hauvette are aware of the alteration.

15. H. de La Ferrière-Percy, *Marguerite d'Angoulême, étude sur ses dernières années* (Paris, 1862). Reproduced also in the Félix Franck edition of the *Marguerites* (Paris, 1873), p. xix.

adages.[16] Hence the name of Dante, as well as the repetition of these phrases, loses much of its significance. It is quite possible that as much may be said for the *guarda e passa* of Hircan; furthermore, the three words of Vergil's counsel reappear in the *Heptaméron* as a detached fragment bearing no relation to their original context. In fact, these meagre allusions to a one-sided Alighieri serve only to destroy the thesis that Marguerite, alone in her century and her country, had understood that poet.

In several of Marguerite's principal poems there are possibilities of Dantesque inspiration. The *Dialogue en forme de vision nocturne*, the first work of the Queen, was composed when she was still Mme L. D. (Duchess of Alençon). In it she used *terza rima*, which only Lemaire des Belges before her had practiced. Meeting her deceased niece Charlotte in a dream or vision, the duchess interrogates her on redemption, faith, and the manner in which "l'amour vous enyvre." The dominating interest in this divine love and its overwhelming effects remind one distantly of the ecstasy and love of the last tercets of the *Paradiso*. Nevertheless, this is hardly a Dantesque vision as some would make it. Only two protagonists are involved. Marguerite admits that she cannot see Charlotte or hear her voice. As for the cosmography of Dante, the aunt pays no heed to it, even when treating the same topics.[17] Interested in the controversies of Erasmus and Luther, Marguerite becomes embroiled in a discussion of free will, a problem clearly resolved in Dante. Although each had a Thomistic education in reference to grace, their points of view here are incompatible. The recurrent fusion of the Rien into the Tout is foreign to the vocabulary of the *Commedia*. Prayers, Mariolatry, ecclesiastical rites, all the impedimenta of Dante's Catholicism are shaken off. If there is an occasional expression

---

16. Farinelli cites the example of a sixteenth-century prisoner who traced on the walls of his cell:

> Il n'a au monde plus grande destresse
> Du bon temps soy souvenir en la tristesse.

In the *Nouvelle revue d'Italie* (Sept.-Oct., 1921), p. 290.

17. Despite the Italian critics,

> Elevez doncques vostre esperit et au rang
> Des bienheureux me voirrez assise,
> Devant mon Dieu, dessus le dextre banc,

harks back to Scripture as readily as to Dante. Compare also Ronsard (Blanchemain edition), I, 245; V, 248.

of a Dantesque turn among the 1293 verses of the *Dialogue,* these are rare; [18] and the basic thought is Lutheran. [19]

It has been stated that Marguerite's use of tercet rime here and elsewhere signifies that she chose the *Commedia* as a model. This form is found not in three, as MM. Comte and Jourda have suggested, [20] but in four of her poems. Her disposition of the rimes is exact, but she differs from Dante in her manipulation of the terminal rimes. This manipulation she did not learn from the ultramontanes Fazio degli Uberti, Serafino, Feo Belcari, and others, for these poets respected and practiced the rime pattern of their master.

Just how does the Queen's versification differ from that of Dante's *terza rima?* One must begin with the *Dialogue,* published in 1533. Thirteen years had elapsed since the appearance of the *Temple de Vénus* and the first *Cupidon et Atropos* of Lemaire, the inaugurator of *terza rima* in France. Marguerite shows her originality by a system which permits her to close her poem without a supplementary verse. The last tercets *xyx, yyz, yyz, yyz* render unnecessary the final quatrain indispensable to Florentine rimes. In the primitive text of the *Navire* [21] one finds a defective series of rimes. Even with the textual revisions of M. Comte [22] one is again far from the final quatrain. Marguerite prefers to create a new order: *xyx, yzy, zyz.* Two occurrences of tercet rime in *la Coche* [23] are perfectly regular, but the third example finishes: *xzx, zyy, z.* The last example, the *Pater Noster,* contains more than 500 continuous lines. [24] The disposition of final verses cor-

---

18. Even Pellegrini concludes by doubting whether one has a right to speak of a Dantesque imitation (*op. cit.,* p. 17). But he, too, would carry the thesis beyond the limits of plausibility. Evidently reading *congnue* for *incongnue,* for example, he finds a parallel idea in "Dinanzi a me non fur cose create" and "Amour est dieu séant sur ciel et nue/Devant lequel n'y a chose incongnue."

19. The Protestantism of this and other poems is underlined by Lefranc, in the *Bulletin de l'histoire du Protestantisme français,* XLVI (1897), pp. 18-19. See also W. G. Moore, *La réforme allemande et la littérature française* (Strasbourg, 1930), pp. 194-95.

20. For C. Comte's discussion of the versification of the Queen, see the *Revue de métrique et de versification,* vol. I, no. 3.

21. The MS 24,298 of the Bibliothèque nationale.

22. C. Comte, *op. cit.,* pp. 124-25.

23. *Les Marguerites,* IV, 209-18; 231-34; 246-48.

24. Published by E. Parturier, *Revue de la Renaissance,* V, 180. The blanks on pages 182 and 183 of this text do not indicate a loss of verses, as an inspection of the rime and sense will show.

responds somewhat to that of the *Dialogue: wxy, xyy, zyy, z.*[25]

Lemaire, like Serafino, had followed the orthodox pattern scrupulously. Mellin de Saint-Gelays, with his *Hecatomphile* of 1534, seems to have come a year or two too late to influence Marguerite. Since he was a court favorite, however, the Queen may have read his poems before their publication. Mellin, like Lemaire, follows carefully the rules set down by the Florentines, but breaks away from them in his *Léger chapitre pour le luth.*[26] There may be reason to believe that it was Saint-Gelays who taught Marguerite her unconventional manipulation of *terza rima.*

Can one agree with any conviction, then, that Marguerite learned her use of this versification from Dante? The reply is negative. One cannot establish that an Italian source[27] was any more probable than a French one; indeed, a French source seems more likely, despite the affirmations of French and Italian scholars already mentioned.[28]

Le petit oeuvre dévot et contemplatif, that important part of the *Pater Noster faict en translation & dialogue*[29] deserves consideration because of the number of striking borrowings from the *Inferno* that it yields, although the tone remains Protestant, if not Lutheran. After paraphrasing the Pater Noster (as in *Purgatorio* XI), Marguerite begins the account of her Christian initiation. She finds herself in the great desert of "folle accoustumance" and hears the voice of reason ("considération"), just as Dante encounters reason "in the great desert."[30] Her "jeune affection" had brought her, like Dante, to a "forêt de peu de cognoissance."[31] But the similar imagery is not maintained throughout the poem. Marguerite abandons the tableau of the *Inferno,* and the allegory becomes a *complaincte* laden with the commonplaces which have become the trade-marks of her thought; impatience with earthly life, hope for early death, desire for union with the Tout-Dieu. One may reasonably assume that she felt

25. An irregularity possibly explained by the later addition of some apocryphal Catholic verses to a poem otherwise Protestant.

26. P. 36 of the edition of 1574.

27. M. Renaudet tells us that his suggestion that it may have been Petrarch (*loc. cit.*) is purely conjectural.

28. No other characteristic of form indicates a definite source. The usual "capitoli" or "chapitres" are lacking. The introduction of both couplet and tercet rime in the same poem Lemaire had practiced.

29. See note 24.

30. *Inferno,* I, 64.

31. P. Jourda, *op. cit.* I, 374, cites several such similarities.

the influence of Dante in her opening pages, and that this influence checked her "talent of effusion." But only in the introduction, for once the poem leaves the Dantesque framework, not
even the restrictions of the tercet rime can keep Marguerite from
her habitual *cacoethes loquendi*. After the entry of the Hoary
Elder, reminiscences of the *Comedy* disappear.[32]

Les Prisons is the poem which Lefranc claims to be the master work of the Queen and which, according to Jourda,[33] is inspired by the *Romance of the Rose* and by Dante. It was from
Dante, Jourda explains, that the Queen borrowed the idea of the
slow and sure ascent of her prisoner toward the supreme good.
Certain traits are undoubtedly common to this poem and the
Inferno. Both are visions; both describe the pilgrimage of an
affranchised prisoner toward his God, the aid of an otherworldly
cicerone, three tyrannical passions to overcome. But the essential
differences are even more marked. These are not the prisons mentioned by Dante.[34]

The first book, or prison, suggests the *Commedia* only in a
passing reference to "le souvenir du mal passé."[35] It is in the
second book that the young poet describes his triumph over the
three beasts of Dante. Rejoicing in the new liberty which the
rupture of his bonds of love has accorded him, he meets the
Amateur de Science, whom Lefranc accepts as Vergil, and others
as Cato of the *Purgatorio*.[36] Despite the allegations of these latter
scholars, the physical appearance of Dante's Cato of Utica[37] has
nothing in common with that of the Amateur de Science. Nor
is there any indication that Marguerite had the Mantuan in mind,
even though the functions of these spiritual counselors are similar,

32. Paradoxically, those who were most ready to read Dante into these
religious poems (Farinelli, Hauvette, Pellegrini, Garosci, and even Renaudet)
neglect this important text completely, although published in 1904, and despite the fact that it and the *Prisons* are the poems closest to Dante.

33. Jourda, *op. cit.* I, 606; Farinelli, *op. cit.* I, 350.

34. *Inf.* X, 56; *Purg.* I, 41; XXIII, 103. H. Hauvette, *Etudes sur la Divine
Comédie*, p. 178; Farinelli, *Dante e la Francia*, I, 354; and later, Jourda, I,
574, have observed that the concentric circles of these three prisons are analogous
to those not of the *Inferno*, but of the *Paradiso*. Yet, Marguerite's last prison,
with its pillars of books, is no more encompassing than her prison of love. Also,
the spirit of the *Paradiso* has nothing in common with the terrestrial prisons
of the Queen.

35. P. 141.

36. A. Lefranc, *Dernières poésies*, p. lvi; Hauvette, *Etudes*, p. 182; Garosci,
Margherita di Navarra, p. 331.

37. *Purg.* I, 37-39.

making Lefranc's hypothesis the more plausible. Among the lengthy recommendations of the old man[38] there is still another commentary on the *nessun maggior dolore*.[39] It is possible that Marguerite thought of the *Inferno* while describing her prisons as "l'abisme infernalle où mon soleil n'apparoissoit." And if, as Jourda says,[40] her "immortelle tristesse" is a paraphrase of the *eterno dolore*, there is an even more direct translation further on: "ny de l'éternelle douleur."[41] The second book of the *Prisons* closes with the direct mention of Dante listed above.

When M. Doumic describes this poem as "litanies of a devout soul, ravished in the admiration of its God,"[42] it is to the third book that he alludes particularly. If the Poet invites his mistress to soar with him toward the heights of wisdom (so that an analogy has been made here with the ascent of Dante and Beatrice in the *Paradiso*), there remain obvious objections. First, there is no such symmeteorisis; the lady refuses to soar. Secondly, the idea that the self-betterment of the individual is an "elevation" is one of the paraphernalia of all moral theorizing. Lastly, the internal evidence of this rise of the individual's Rien toward the Tout belies any such hypothesis. Although the God into whom Marguerite's nothingness is to "melt" is trinitarian,[43] it is both a quasi-Platonic Idea and a Protestant, antilibertarian deity, and it is obvious that she is "concluding with Luther and not with Dante," to quote M. Renaudet.[44] One finds, then, in this poem of heroic proportions many incontestable evocations of the *Inferno*, even if the tone is Protestant, but hardly so many as some critics claim.[45] To support their thesis that Marguerite borrowed heavily from Dante, scholars have had recourse principally to this poem which, thanks to the allegory of the three beasts, seemed the most fruitful of results.

After an examination of the *Prisons*, *la Navire* offers few influences or analogies. The fact that this work is in tercet rime

---

38. If Jourda (*op. cit.*, I, 568) believes after Farinelli that a couplet of this episode and one of *la Navire* are similar to the "inferma che non puo trovar posa" of *Purg.* VI, 110, it is hardly conclusive. Much closer to Marguerite is Ronsard's use of this image (Blanchemain edition, IV, 309).

39. P. 174.

40. *Loc. cit., note* 38.

41. P. 205.

42. R. Doumic, *Revue des deux mondes*, t. 133, p. 944.

43. P. 293.

44. A. Renaudet, *Revue du seizième siècle*, 1931, p. 297.

45. As, for example, Garosci, *Margherita di Navarra*, 331 and *passim*.

might promise some resemblance with the ideas of Dante, for the other passages in tercets, like the *Dialogue* and the *Petit Oeuvre,* have occasionally yielded them. Here the ship or vessel in question is the soul of the Queen troubled by the death of her brother, a ship "grounded far from the tranquil haven of faith and hope." This is an image that Dante uses to describe the deviation of a Christian,[46] although in no such way as to suggest it to the Queen. In this work, as in the *Dialogue,* a deceased relative returns in a dream to become, in Lefranc's words, "auprès d'elle le défenseur des opinions qu'il (François) persécutait de son vivant." The Queen, once again in a desert comparable to the desert of the *Inferno,* receives information and consolation from her vision. Hauvette admits that it is mainly *form* that the Queen derives here from Dante, and adds that it is the metrical form, the imagery, and the "allure génerale" that will link these verses with the *Commedia.*[47] As for the metrical form, which is very defective in the manuscript, we have shown that her manipulation of *terza rima* cannot be attributed to Dante. The words lack economy and the images lack precision, while the general "allure" seems rather that of a Protestant document.

The voice which comes to succour the wayward sinner is no longer the same evocation of Vergil which some found in the recital of the Queen's conversion. Here no verse seems taken from Dante. Until the end the brother remains only an incorporeal voice. Even the emotional crises are of a different nature; Dante's resulting from a spiritual *traviamento* and Marguerite's from an excess of bereavement. Francis I appears here, not to point out the way to affranchisement of the will, as did Vergil, but simply to console. Gaston Paris said that one ought to entitle this the "Consolation of Francis First." However, even if one were to conceive that this framework was vaguely inspired by the beginning of the *Inferno,* such a concession would coincide readily with one of the conclusions that these pages are shaping, i.e., that Marguerite knew only the first few cantos of the *Comedy.* It seems hardly admissible, however, that the ascent of Francis

46. *Purg.* VI, 77; XVII, 78.

47. Hauvette, *Etudes,* pp. 173, 175; Farinelli, *op. cit.* I, 345-46: "Giammai terzine scritte in lingua di Francia ritrassero il vigoroso spirito di Dante come quelle." Jourda, *op. cit.* I, 567: "(on) peut écrire avec Farinelli que l'apparition de François Ier à Marguerite dans la *Navire* rappelle celle de Virgile à Dante, et que l'ascension du Roi au ciel fait songer à celle de Béatrice et de l'Alighieri au chant II du Paradis."

toward the clouds recalls that of Dante and Beatrice in *Paradiso* II.[48]

There is a reference to the *nessun maggior dolore* in the lines on the cruelty of memory.[49] Beyond this there are no echoes of Dante. The paradise of which Francis makes his report is a Protestant heaven. Moreover, the ethical problems and casuistry of mediaeval theology have little attraction for Marguerite. To her, these are "fascheulx debatz." Briefly, this masterpiece in Florentine rime, whatever one may say of it, is further from the spirit of Dante than the *Dialogue*, the *Petit Oeuvre*, or the *Prisons*.

Of the Queen's other works, collected in the *Marguerites*[50] or scattered through various journals, little remains to be said. After having edited the "Pater Noster" in the *Revue de la Renaissance*, Parturier adds several rondeaux attributable to the Queen. Two especially are of interest for the Dante scholar. The first is that printed by La Ferrière-Percy (see note 24). Both refer to the Francesca episode, which apparently remained long in Marguerite's memory. The second example that we have found is:

> Et lors j'auray pour douleur plus amère
> Me recorder au temps de la misère
> De l'heur passé de ma félicité. . . .[51]

The Oraison de Nostre Seigneur Jésus-Christ" offers nothing for our particular investigation; nor is Dante reflected in the "Miroir de l'âme pécheresse." As for the "Triomphe de l'ag-

48. The departure of the brother (alone) occupies only a few brief lines, three of which Farinelli cites to support his argument. However, an examination of the texts makes it difficult to accept the tercet:

> La nue blanche, ainsy que naige fine,
> Entre nous deux se mist et emporta
> Ceste ame au ciel toute claire et divine.

as an imitation of *Par.* II, 31-32:

> Pareva a me che nube ne coprisse
> Lucida, spessa, solida e polita.

49. P. 393.

50. *Les Marguerites de la Marguerite des Princesses*, edited by F. Franck (Paris, 1873), 4 vols.

51. A slightly different treatment of the *nessun dolore* is found in one of the sections of "la Coche" where tercet rime is used:

> Hélas, jugez en quel travail je suis!
> Je n'ay plus rien, sinon que la mémoire
> Du bien passé, qui entretient mon deuil.

See also, the *Navire*, p. 393: "Au temple heureux de cruel souvenir."

neau," the beautiful poem on redemption, to assert that the ascent of the lamb derives from that of Dante and Beatrice, as has been claimed, and not from Golgotha itself, is wishful scholarship. The ingenious punishments of the "thousand little hells" that Marguerite lists[52] are very different from the torments of the *Inferno*. Jourda suggests that "the idea of painting the glory of Christ (here) came to the Queen from a reading of the *Commedia*."[53] And Farinelli, noting that the tone here is more lyrical than usual, attributes this to Dante.[54] Yet all majestic or grave composition of Marguerite is not inspired by Dante. In fact, the tone of the "Triomphe" is more evangelical than anything else. Jourda himself admits as notable sources the Apocalypse, the Epistles to the Ephesians and to the Romans.

One fact remains in opposition to those who have assumed that the ascendancy of Dante over Marguerite's thought was a considerable one. Marguerite, the Pearl of the Valois, approved of the Reformation. If the poor Queen was annoyed by the "fascheulx debatz" of the Reformers as well as of the Roman fathers, she remains no less Reformist herself.[55] Wherever she treats of the cult of the saints, redemption, grace, and the like, she is no longer an orthodox Catholic. Not only is she uninterested in the theological side of the *Commedia*; she is opposed to it as well.

Nevertheless, the *Commedia* contains, in addition to a theology, the story of an errant pilgrim making his way toward his God. When Marguerite thought of Dante she thought of the straying sinner of the first cantos of the *Inferno*, and seemed to enjoy identifying herself with him each time she found herself in a mortal desert akin to his: thus, the first scenes of the *Petit Oeuvre*, the *Dialogue en forme de vision nocturne*, the *Navire*, and the second book of the *Prisons*. Each of these four poems shows the same recidivism. It is always the same moral crisis of the wayward pilgrim, the same subjection to vice from which she frees herself with a Dantesque effort of will. Then, once her poem gathers momentum under more personal inspiration, she forgets her master and returns to her own type of Protestant mysticism, characterized by a will to die—as insistent as her

---

52. P. 31.

53. Jourda, *op. cit.* I, 338.

54. Farinelli, *op. cit.* I, 338.

55. A. Lefranc concludes (see note 19, above) that "ces œuvres sont inspirées d'un bout à l'autre par le plus pur esprit protestant."

contemporary Saint Teresa's *muero que no muero*—the same conviction of her own nothingness, the same effusions of love verse to the God-Spouse. If in the *Prisons* she returns to the inspired idea of the *Commedia*, the meeting with God and the fusion of her will with the Creator's, this return shows that many roads lead to God, without always passing through Rome. The royal road of the Queen generally detours through Meaux.

Preparing these conclusions, we have examined not only borrowings from the *Commedia* but many verses which have a Dantesque turn. It is interesting to group the possible parallels of verses and passages according to their disposition into the first, second, or third books of the *Commedia*, basing the statistics on our own and others' investigations.

	Inferno	Purgatorio	Paradiso
Specific borrowings	21	0	0
Possible borrowings	12	5	8

All incontrovertible borrowings, then, are from the first book of the *Commedia*, with apparently none from the *Convivio* or the *Rime*. Furthermore, of the plagiarisms from the *Inferno*, all are from the first five cantos. Even the majority of the verses with Dantesque imagery or phraseology are from these first five cantos. One understands, then, why Dante remained for Marguerite "celuy qui nous vient icy peindre son triste enfer." Nowhere in the poetic works of the Queen have we found a verse that is incontestably a plagiarism from the *Purgatorio* or the *Paradiso*. Sometimes an image has seemed to derive from these two books, *e.g.*, "gratter la rogne," "navire assablée," "citoyenne serez de ma cité"; but in no case are the two contexts similar.

From the preceding paragraphs one may understand why Marguerite's borrowings were restricted to the first cantos of the *Inferno*. As we have seen, the Queen was interested in the personal character of the poem, and it is in the *Inferno's* exordium that the ethos of its author is most succinctly depicted. Dante is here a mortal, *triste* and *ennuyé*, halfway along life's highroad. In fact, all of the direct mentions of Dante's name in Marguerite's works are inspired by these five cantos. If the Lover of the *Prisons* counsels the reading of "tout le discours de Dante," he does not appear to have persevered to such an extent himself. It would seem that the verse at the close of Canto V, "quel giorno più non vi leggemmo avante," exercised such power of suggestion upon the Queen that at this point she laid down the *Commedia* for good.

Another reason for the multiplicity of references to the proemial part of the *Inferno* is Marguerite's repetition of certain favorite verses which occur in this part. The *nessun maggior dolore* is the most remarkable example. Another possible explanation is that the opening of the *Inferno* contains more graphic and polychromatic passages in close succession than the rest of the epic. Later, when the human and the awesome qualities of the poem are subordinated to discussions of a philosophical or theological nature, Marguerite will cry, as usual, "fascheulx debatz." Add to this a distaste for scholastic dialectic and casuistry, which her mysticism forbade her, even if that of Dante suffered it, as well as an ignorance of the real thought and purposes of the Italian poet. If she started out to read the *Commedia* with an exegesis, as the allegory of the three beasts indicates, she soon wearied of this method of study. By the circumstantial evidence of her poetic works, one may conclude that Marguerite knew only the protasis of the *Inferno* and perhaps the mystical crisis which terminates the *Paradiso*. Like a good Lutheran, she ignores purgatory completely.

During her entire life Marguerite was subject to visions. It was in a vision that she learned of the death of her brother. As the masterpiece of Dante was an intuitive vision,[56] it was admissible that it contributed toward her taste for and technic of visions. Thus, while approaching one of her ecstatic perceptions, she seems to start along Dantean paths, using this poet as cicerone. But if the mystiques of these two poets are based on vision, intuition, and contemplation, they present different characteristics, Dante awaiting the assimilation of his will with that of the impersonal High Maker, Marguerite longing for a fusion of her Rien with that Tout which she calls her "spouse, lover, father, brother, and son." This is a language which Dante never permitted himself in the *Commedia*,[57] just as he took care to avoid the pantheistic images of preceding centuries.

What Marguerite might best have learned from the master work of the Trecento she failed to learn: the clear, simple, well-developed style which Dante bequeathed to the Italians, just as her contemporary Calvin left his to the French. The different characters of the two poets, one cerebral and one exclusively pathic, so to speak, explain the divergence of their styles. If Marguerite at rare moments attains a Dantesque clarity and

56. *Par.* XXXIII, 62.
57. Purely conventional are *Par.* X, 141-42; *Inf.* XXIV, 5.

simplicity, her style remains essentially (the euphemism is Tilley's) prolix. As Lanson said of Jean de Meun, "Parentheses of 500 verses cost the author nothing."

A noteworthy fact is suggested by the *Dialogue*, the *Petit Oeuvre*, the *Prisons*, and the *Navire*; in these the Queen employs the device of substituting herself for Dante, giving herself the rôle of sinner in the desert or the forest. It is precisely here that the form of the poetry most closely recalls Dante. In the *Prisons*, while thinking of the inferno of Dante, she identifies herself with Dante, her alter ego; hence it is natural for her to versify in tercets. Even the brief passage in tercet rime of the *Coche* contains a Dantesque remembrance. When the Queen is thinking of Dante, she reveals it in her manner of writing; thus one is entitled to conclude that she thought of Dante rarely. And upon those rare occasions when she did, it was hardly a Dante Alighieri that Professor Zingarelli would have recognized.

VIII

RONSARD, MICHELANGELO, AND THREE "INEDITA" FROM BURY

I T IS RECORDED that Pierre de Ronsard composed three poems in honor of statuary assembled by the powerful patron Florimond Robertet in the Château de Bury, near Blois. The attribution of these verses to Ronsard leaves questions to be answered and there has been no Ronsard scholar who has taken them seriously enough to discuss them. The two poems occasioned by marble figures of Porcia and of Ptolemy hold some interest for us because they treat of historical themes not encountered elsewhere in the canzoniere of Ronsard, and in any case themes rare in Renaissance poetry and tragedy. The third piece, presented as a Ronsard translation from Michelangelo, may shed light—whoever the translator—on a mystery which has resisted scholarship for centuries.

In the year 1650 Henri Chesneau, poet, advocate, and retainer of Messire Charles, Marquis et Comte de Rostaing, brought out a volume entitled *Bury Rostaing,* whose principal objective was to exalt the dynasty of the aforementioned Florimond Robertet ("le Grand"), Baron d'Alluye, de Bury et de Brou, and great-grandfather of Messire Charles on his maternal side. An important section of *Bury Rostaing* consisted of an inventory of the furnishing and art objects present in the Château de Bury shortly after the death of Florimond († 1527).[1] As only one known copy of *Bury Rostaing* has survived in recent times, the possessor of that copy, Eugène Grésy, felt that this defective impression of 266 pages and thirteen *planches,* with its faulty pagination and penned corrigenda, was never given a full press run. Since both the original inventory and Chesneau's reprint of it in *Bury Rostaing* had vanished, with the exception of the unique copy mentioned, Grésy proceeded to publish the census in the *Mémoirs de la Sociéte impériale des Antiquaires de France* in 1868, prefacing the text with a statement on Chesneau's relations with the Robertet family but leaving many questions still to be

---

1. Two French and one Spanish encyclopedias set this date at 1522, a date disproved by Robertet's role after Pavia and by available correspondence: *Lettres de Marguerite d'Angoulême* (Paris, 1841), p. 465, where Robertet is still being wished a long and happy life in 1525.

posed concerning the inventory.[2] The cataloguer probably was, as Chesneau claimed, Florimond's widow, Mme. Michelle Gaillard de Longjumeau, since the compiler not only lists the objects but usually supplies detailed explanations about their provenience. The year to which Chesneau assigned this compilation is 1532, a dating which is at the core of the "Ronsard problem" presented in this essay.

After Veuve Robertet has made a careful perquisition of the jewels, furnishings, tapestries, paintings, and other treasures of Bury, she arrives at length at the marble statues. Here is the distraught Porcia, crushed by the suicides of her father Cato Uticensis and her husband Brutus and "s'éteignant la vie avec des charbons ardents." No details are supplied about this or other statues. Whether Porcia is swallowing live coals or suffocating herself with the smoke (both versions were current) we do not know. The pathetic figure of this loyal wife and participant in her husband's conspiracies moved the poet—supposedly Ronsard —to set down the following twelve verses, which sound like the recital of the chorus after the last turning-point of a neo-classic tragedy ("Aussi Ronsard en a-t-il encores fait ces douze vers"):

> Porcie n'ayant plus son grand Caton d'Utique
>   Ny son très cher Brutus,
> Conclut résolument une mort héroique
>   Pour finir ses vertus.
> Mon père et mon mary, disoit-elle sans cesse
>   Eurent l'esprit si fort
> Que ne pouvant se voir dans l'extreme foiblesse,
>   Ils se mirent à mort.
> Et moy tout ainsi qu'eux ne pouvant pas permettre
>   Que l'on me fit souffrir,
> Je previns les rigueurs de l'un et l'autre sceptre,
>   En me faisant mourir.[3]

Although the alternance of ten-syllabics with six-syllabics was common enough in Ronsard, the versification here is not typical. In fact, the metric scheme would be just as unusual for any other poet as for Ronsard, as Kastner notes: "Scarcely more common

2. Eugène Grésy, "Inventaire des objets d'art comprenant la succession de Florimond Robertet, ministre de François Ier, dressé par sa veuve," *Mémoires de la Société impériale des Antiquaires de France*, 3e série, tome X (Paris, 1868), 1-66.

3. *Ibid.*, p. 55.

is the form in which Alexandrines and lines of six syllables alternate on cross rimes."[4]

The following figure in the census is a marble of "Ptolemy, King of Egypt and most learned in astrology." Writes the compiler of the census, "Je ne veux pas manquer de mettre icy les vers que le jeune Gentilhomme Pierre Ronsard fit, il y a quelques jours, en considérant cette digne figure:

> Pleust à Dieu que les Roys establissent les vogues,
> Qu'eux et leurs successeurs devinssent Astrologues,
> Pour prevoir les desseins et les mauvais projects,
> Que les determinez font contre leurs sujects:
> Afin qu'en sçachant tout ainsi que Ptolemée,
> Rien ne nuisit aux biens ny à la Renommée."[5]

The metric pattern and couplet rime are of course typical enough of Ronsard, as is this belief in the efficacy of astrology. In his "Hymne des astres," his "Hymne des estoiles," and elsewhere, he shows a greater tolerance for astral divination than did his contemporaries.[6] It is curious that the successful reign of Ptolemy I, secure against the "designs and evil plans" of Syria, Cyprus, and other potential enemies, should be viewed as benefitting from astrology, since under Ptolemy and his son Ptolemy Philadelphus more strides were made in astronomy than at any other period of history.

The third poem allegedly by Ronsard is the reported translation from Michelangelo, the background of which must be explained. As is known, Michelangelo's bronze *David* was executed on commission for Pierre de Rohan, Maréchal de Gié and powerful favorite of Louis XII. After Rohan's headlong fall from royal favor in 1504, when the statue was still unfinished in Florence, his fellow councilor of state, Florimond Robertet—who could have given Machiavelli lessons on how to stay at the helm of government during one reign after another—maneuvered to procure the statue for himself. In 1509 he set it up in his Hôtel d'Alluye at Blois and shortly thereafter had it placed on a pedestal in the center of the courtyard of his recently completed familial castle, the Château de Bury. That it remained there for many decades is known, for it is visible in the elevation of the château and gardens drawn by Jacques Androuet

4. L. E. Kastner, *History of French Versification* (Oxford, 1903), p. 217.
5. Grésy, *op cit.*, p. 55.
6. See R. J. Clements, *Critical Theory and Practice of the Pléiade* (Cambridge, Mass., 1942), pp. 220-26.

Du Cerceau in 1576.[7] Veuve Robertet's inventory tells us that there were several lines in Italian at the base of the statue, inscribed by Michelangelo himself. The census states: "Et faisons aussi beaucoup d'estat des vers Italiens que Miquel-Ange, statuaire de ce chef-d'oeuvre, fit graver au pied d'estal et que le sçavant Ronsard a traduicts en ce sens:

> Moy David en moins de trois pas,
> Que je fis devant tout le monde,
> Je mis Goliat au trespas
> D'un seul juste coup de ma fronde,
> Et de ma harpe je fis voir
> Qu'avec la charmente Muzique
> L'on repousse tout le pouvoir
> De la ruse diabolique."[8]

There is no echo of Michelangelo's many poems in all the published works of Ronsard, nor of his art. Other references to David in Ronsard's poetry concern the Hebrew hero later in life, as king. No mention is made of the young liberator and singer of songs.

An inconsistency must be explained away if these three poems are to be attributed to Ronsard, who was born on 11 September 1524. The inventory containing these poems was said by Chesneau to have been compiled by the widow Robertet on 4 August 1532. One's immediate reaction, as was that of my old master Paul Laumonier,[9] is that these stanzas could not have come from the pen of Ronsard. This conclusion occurred also to Grésy, who wrote in a footnote that Ronsard "n'aurait eu que huit ans lorsqu'il composa ce sixain inédit." Indeed, he had not yet reached his eighth birthday. Although accepting the date of 1532 as accurate and noting the chronological dilemma, Grésy expressed no surprise that Madame Robertet could have known of Ronsard's existence in that year or that she could have felt gratification over a poem written "a few days ago" by Ronsard. Obviously the poems and consequently the inventory in its published version are of a later date, when "the young gentleman Pierre Ronsard" had established some degree of reputation. That moment could not have preceded 1550, the year of the first *Odes et Bocage*. Since the date of 1532 falls under suspicion, only

7. Jacques Androuet Du Cerceau, *Les plus excellents bâtiments de France* (1576), p. 125.
8. Grésy, *op. cit.*, p. 59.
9. Laumonier-Lemerre edition of Ronsard (Paris, 1914-19), VI, 508.

two explanations are possible. First, Mme. Robertet's census was definitely composed or terminated about 1550. Second, Chesneau or some knowledgeable third party between 1532 and 1650 embroidered upon the text of the inventory before it was edited. Since the original manuscript has been lost, there is no way of verifying which of these explanations is the more likely. If one of them is valid, then we are possibly in the presence of three interesting poems by Ronsard, less competent or mature than others but distinctive in theme. If neither explanation is valid, the purported translation from Michelangelo loses none of its interest for the light it sheds upon his attitude toward one of his finest creations.

For the moment, let us assume with the record that Ronsard wrote these strophes. From the chronology of his friendships with the descendants of the great Florimond Robertet, Ronsard could have frequented the Château de Bury, the Hôtel d'Alluye, and other properties of the family from about 1550 to 1569, year of the death of Robertet d'Alluye. In the *Nouvelles poésies* of 1563 the grandson and grandnephew respectively of Florimond le Grand, the Baron Florimond Robertet d'Alluye and Robertet Seigneur de Fresne, appear in a pastoral as Aluyot and Fresnet.[10] In this same year Ronsard dedicated *Hymnes* ("Hymne du printemps," "Hymne de l'esté") to these same friends.[11] The durability of Ronsard's affection for the Robertet family is shown as late as 1584 in an ode where he replaces the name of Revergat with the name of Robertet de Fresne.[12]

Whether or not marble figures of Porcia and Ptolemy were removed to other accessible family properties before or after 1576, the *David* was still standing in the courtyard that year, as attested by the Du Cerceau sketch. Who carved these statues of a patrician woman and a Greek soldier turned king, generally neglected as subjects by Renaissance painters and sculptors? Although the inventory names other artists when they are outstanding (a hitherto unknown painted *Pietà* by Michelangelo turns up!)[13] it does not identify the artists in question, and we must assume that they were minor sculptors. In any case, the marble figures have been dispersed and lost. The chateau itself was allowed by the family to fall into disrepair and ruin within

10. Pierre de Ronsard, *Œuvres complètes* (Paris, STFM, 1946), XII, 93.
11. *Ibid.*, pp. 27, 35.
12. Paul Laumonier, *Ronsard poète lyrique* (Paris, 1923), p. 131.
13. Grésy, *op. cit.*, pp. 39-40.

a hundred years, thus serving as an unhappy demonstration of
Ronsard's prediction about those who lavish money on castles:

> Bufles, qui aiment mieux faire grande leur race
> Ou bastir des Palais, que d'acquerir la grace
> D'Apollon: ô les sots, qui ne cognoissent pas
> Qu'à la fin leurs chasteaux trebucheront à bas,
> Et qu'en moins de cent ans leurs races incognues
> Se traineront sans nom par les tourbes menues.[14]

The fact that we no longer have either the statues or the original
manuscript of the census against which to check Ronsard's poetry
illustrates another text of Ronsard:

> Mais Dieu ne le veut pas, qui couvre soubz la terre
> Tant de livres perdus, naufrages de la guerre,
> Tant d'ars laborieux.[15]

As we shall see below, the bronze *David* disappeared as completely as did the marble figures. All that remains to communicate the
messages of the sculptors are the three poems purportedly by
Ronsard, a reminder of the *scripta manent* theme so prominent
in the writings of this poet: "faisant un vers plus durable / Qu'un
Colosse elabouré."[16]

As the initial pages of this book endeavored to illustrate, the
Renaissance was the period which saw the *ut pictura poesis* expand
from an obscure and restricted five lines in Horace into a quasi-
philosophical awareness of the identical aims and processes of
painting and poetry. Naturally, painters were imitating poems
and illustrating scenes from contemporary epics, romances, and
pastorals: typical were the paintings of Tasso's Rinaldo and Armida by Carracci, Finoglio, and Tiepolo.[17] Less to be expected
was the extent to which poets imitated or modelled verse upon
contemporary painting and sculpture. Earlier we have cited instances of this among poems by Giovanni Strozzi, Jacopo Sadole-
to, Venegas de Saavedra, and Soto de Rojas. It would be pleasant
to think that Ronsard lent the prestige of his name to this endeavor.

The uncovering of the poems to Porcia and Ptolemy is of interest mainly to *ronsardisants*. The pieces are pleasant exercises,

14. Ronsard, *ed. cit.*, VIII, 292, variant of 1587.
15. *Ibid.*, VIII, 357.
16. *Ibid.*, II, 89.
17. Rensselaer W. Lee, "*Ut Pictura Poesis:* The Humanistic Theory of
Painting," *Art Bulletin*, XXII (December, 1940), pp. 242-50: contains a most
interesting study of the pictorial treatment of Tasso's Rinaldo and Armida.

one of them metrically unusual, even if they do not attain the most mature levels of Ronsard's production. Let us now assume, however, that it was not Ronsard, but a later poet (or poetess) attached to the Robertet family, who did the composition and translation under question. As stated above, the translation from Michelangelo remains of utmost importance to the student of fine arts, whether it was done by some prince of poets named Ronsard or some other poet lost in oblivion, perhaps even Du Chesneau, who dabbled in verse (see below).

First of all, were the Italian verses at the base of the bronze *David* written by Michelangelo, as the inventory attests, or by someone else? This question occurs to the student of Michelangelo, Anatole de Montaiglon. "Il pouvait y avoir des vers italiens sur la base de la colonne sans qu'ils fussent pour cela de Michel-Ange."[18] The inscription would not have been found on the column, by the way, but rather on the base or dado at the foot of the statue and crowning the column; the underpinning marble column seen in the Du Cerceau drawing did not in fact come from Italy with the bronze, since it was agreed that no *fornimento* would be sent.[19] If an Italian poem by some one other than Michelangelo were inscribed on the dado, it would be unique among Buonarroti's productions and certainly done without his knowledge or consent.

It is difficult to confirm or deny the presence of a poem by Michelangelo on the dado or base of this lost *David*. There is no mention of such a poem or inscription in the vast literature on Michelangelo or in the various published collections of his canzoniere. Yet such a poem probably existed. To begin with, there is the general reliability of the inventory set up by the Robertet family, descendants of Florimond Robertet, a man so powerful in France that in the words of Commynes he governed the country in the name of his monarchs. Then, too, it was in keeping with Michelangelo's practice to set down a poem lending the gift of speech to one of his statues. In one of his *Rime*, the *Notte* of the Medici Chapel deplored conditions in Florence after the Medici restoration. Another piece in free verse lets us listen to his *Giorno* and *Notte* speculating on what Giuliano de' Medici might have accomplished had he not died prematurely.

18. Anatole de Montaiglon, *Gazette des Beaux-Arts*, deuxième série, XIII (1876), 245.

19. Charles de Tolnay, *The Youth of Michelangelo* (Princeton, 1943), p. 207.

In another stanza his stone effigy of Cecchino de' Bracci regrets having come down from his lofty mountain top. The whole concept of the living, breathing, and talking stone was familiar to Buonarroti.[20]

That Michelangelo was perhaps at the very outset planning such a poem to accompany this bronze statue may be adduced from a mysterious distich (or hendecasyllabic line) accompanying the Louvre pen sketch of the bronze *David* and the right arm of the marble *David*. (See the frontispiece of the present volume.) This scholium reads

> Dauicte cholla fromba
> e io choll' archo
> Michelagniolo[21]

For years students have been unable to agree on the meaning of this distich or even to explain its presence alongside the sketches of 1501 or 1502. We will not review here the many conjectural interpretations or enter into the disputed points of iconography, but simply point out that the burden of the distich most generally accepted is that David serves God as triumphantly with his sling as Michelangelo does with his art.

The inventory which finally appeared in *Bury Rostaing* helps to clarify this mysterious scholium. Around 1502, the date assigned to the distich and signature, Michelangelo must have toyed with the idea of placing on the base of the bronze *David* not only his signature or name but also an inscription or strophe establishing the personal relationship between himself and this figure. The intimate rapport existing between the artist and the work of art he had already heralded in another sonnet: "Chom' esser, Donna, può quel c' alcun uede."[22] Heretofore Michelangelo had placed his name, but nothing more, on his creations (*e.g.*, the *Madonna della Febbre*). We assume that he intended his inscription growing out of the scholium to accompany the bronze *David* rather than the marble "giant" (represented by only an arm), since we learn from Vasari and others that the marble

---

20. Michelangelo often refers in his poetry to such concepts as living stone, living figures, living images, and the like: Carl Frey edition of the *Dichtungen*, pp. 480, 194, 157. He apostrophizes the figure of Cecchino de' Bracci as a living being with the faculty of memory ("Tu sol pietra il sai!") and quotes a scornful comment of this figure on his verses: pp. 70, 74.

21. Carl Frey, *Dichtungen des Michelagniolo Buonarroti* (Berlin, 1897), p. 1.

22. *Ibid.*, p. 194.

David was conceived by the municipal authorities as having an exclusively civic symbolism, a meaning upon which an intrusive inscription of a personal nature would have trespassed. The bronze *David*, being done for a private patron, could tolerate such a personal stanza. It is possible to suppose, then, that the distich above is actually a hendecasyllabic line and was to be a part of a poem heralding his statue and identifying himself as an artist and servant of God. The length of the inscription in her courtyard is not revealed by Mme. Robertet or her compilers, and the translation into French need not be conclusive or even informative on this point, since the Renaissance definition of imitation or translation ran the gamut from transverbalization to the most free and loose *innutrition*. (See the third essay in this volume.) Michelangelo, for example, never adopted the octosyllabic line suggested by the translation, even though it was common enough in Ronsard. One must conclude from the French version that the first product of Michelangelo's afflatus metamorphosed into a poem differing from his original intention, as happened so often with his sculpture—a poem from which he withdrew mention of himself as an alter ego of *David* and let the young and triumphant son of Jesse speak only of himself. The *arco* of the scholium then can become *arco* in the sense of harp-frame, and the parallels *fromba-fronde* and *arco-harpe* result. The original theme of David's spiritual and physical strength is retained; mention of his prowess as a musician is introduced. The addition of the element of music, although it had no part in the ideation of the statue, was not foreign to Michelangelo, many of whose madrigals were set to music and who numbered Arcadelt and Tromboncino among his friends.[23] Indeed, just as Saul used to like to listen to the young David playing his harp, so did Michelangelo go to listen to the singing of the young chansonnier Luigi Pulci, grandson of the writer of comic romance.[24]

This emergence of the expanding personality of David in the metamorphosed Italian poem, with the attendant crowding out of Michelangelo, coincides with David's increasingly dominant ego as the conception of the statue itself evolved. In its final stage of evolution the bronze (if one accepts Du Cerceau's drawing) is

23. "Spargendo il senso il ardor cocente" was set to music by Arcadelt and "Com aro dunque ardire" by Tromboncino. See Gaetano Milanesi, *Le Lettere di Michelangelo Buonarroti* (Florence, 1875), p. 480.

24. Benvenuto Cellini, *Vita* (Florence, 1890), p. 79.

informed with the triumphant and dominant note of the lines translated by Ronsard, for unlike the conceptions of the Louvre sketch, or of the callow "Giant" in the corner spandrel of the Sistine Ceiling, this David holds aloft "devant tout le monde" the head of Goliath. As for the details of the transformation of the distich (or hendecasyllable) into the longer translated poem, as for the motivations behind those detailed changes, it is useless to contrive hypotheses from the available data.

Our chance to check the exact nature of that transformation, centered upon the Italian verses at the base of the *David*, disappeared by 1650, when Henri Chesneau penned his poetic description of the Château de Bury:

> Autrefois dans cet endroict même
> Il y avoit un beau David,
> Mais tout-à-coup l'on le ravit
> A cause de son prix extreme . . .
> Tant il est d'une heureuse fonte.[25]

We know that the bronze figure was removed to the Château de Villeroy at Mennecy and had disappeared from that location by mid-century. With it went our last hopes of verifying that Michelangelo Buonarroti brought to full articulation his hermetic thought about David and his sling, a poetic development turned into French, possibly by Ronsard as an amiable gesture to his friends of the *gens* Robertet. The imagination and boldness of Michelangelo's inventions and *concetti* could well have appealed to Ronsard, for it was by this criterion that Du Bellay, who knew something of both men, found Ronsard and Michelangelo kindred spirits.[26]

Historical circumstances would seem to bear out that we possess three unheralded poems of passing interest to Ronsard scholars and one of particular interest to Michelangelo scholars, which has remained unknown to art historians despite the perception it affords of Michelangelo's thought. It is interesting that all three have their ultimate origin in statues from which a lesson in virtue was to be derived: a patrician matron whose nobility of character impels her to share the consequences of death with those two beloved men in whose political beliefs she concurred and whose activities she encouraged; a king whose interest in

---

25. Grésy, *op. cit.*, p. 64.

26. Joachim de Bellay, *Œuvres poétiques* (Paris, 1931) VI, 164-65. In Rome, Du Bellay lived in the Palazzo Farnese when Michelangelo's cornice was being added.

astrology is to make him more clairvoyant about the menaces and evil designs lying in store for his people; a young shepherd who rests secure in the knowledge that the love of God is one's greatest armor. All these effigies of marble and bronze vanished, possibly even in the lifetime of Ronsard, the messages of their sculptors lost forever except as recorded in these poems by the Prince of Poets or a rival of lesser rank:

> Le marbre, ou l'airain vêtu
> D'un labeur vif par l'enclume
> N'animent pas la vertu
> Comme je fai par ma plume.[27]

27. Ronsard, *ed. cit.*, I, 92.

IX

"THE PHILOSOPHIE OF CAVALIERS"

THE RENAISSANCE cult of the Gentleman had its own hagiography, starting way back with the knightly Cadmus, son of Agenor, who brought culture from Phoenicia to Europe and made "civilized men of boors," as the emblem writer Alciati put it.[1] Its golden legend included great names from Hector down to Pierre Terrail, without fear and without reproach, who as the Chevalier Bayard knighted his own monarch on the battlefield, and Baldassare Castiglione at whose death Carlos Quinto sighed, "I tell you that one of the finest gentlemen in the world has passed away." The cult had its sacred books, the earliest of which was the *Aeneid*, which taught polished Augustan manners, in opposition to the uncouth society depicted in the *Odyssey* and the *Iliad*.[2] The cult was abundantly provided with catechisms, drawn up by such high priests as Stefano Guazzo, Giovanni della Casa, Thomas Lyly, Richard Braithwaite, and Castiglione himself, author of the *Cortegiano*. The French catechisms and *regulae* came later: Du Souhait's *Parfaict Gentilhomme* in 1600, Nicolas Pasquier's *Gentilhomme* in 1611, and Nicolas Faret's *Honneste homme* in 1630. The cult also had its own iconography, as we shall show below.

It is by way of a paradox that whereas the manuals on civility were less numerous in France of the sixteenth century than in Italy, England, or even Spain, the gentlemanly way of life was as highly codified and observed as anywhere by the inhabitants of such architectural masterpieces as Azay-le-Rideau and Chenonceaux. In France courtliness was borne along not so much by treatises as by letters, memoirs, paternal or priestly counsels, traditions, written and unwritten laws. An entrenched sense of correctness kept gentlemen and commoners apart and assigned separate mores to each class. If a gentleman rode up to the scene of a duel, for example, his mount was confiscated by the marshals; if a commoner rode alongside to watch, he lost an ear. Lest the newly-rich bourgeois dress and adorn himself like a nobleman, "edicts had to be passed from time to time to prevent him from looking too much like a gentleman."

1. Andrea Alciati, *Emblemata* (Paris, 1589), p. 640.
2. The contrast between the civilized Vergil and the primitive Homer comes out clearly in Scaliger's discussion of the epic in his *Poetics*.

In a brilliant and readable book on the Renaissance gentleman W. L. Wiley sheds light on the whole question of gentility and civility in France, a tradition which he claims was more short-lived than we have expected.[3] "The Renaissance gentleman really came into being in the few years leading up to the coronation of Francis I in 1515, and he expired in the civil strife that broke out in the 1560's during the reign of Charles IX." If one objects that after the 1560's there were some extremely important courtesy books—by Timotei, Muzio, Ascham, Peacham, Du Souhait, Nervèse, and others—Wiley's answer is that at least in France these tended to teach one to get along at court rather than to live up to a code of gentility. His second, and to us more cogent, answer is that changing political and socio-economic conditions prevented the golden age of the Gentleman from extending past the sixteenth century.

To be sure, the question which Wiley explores is a tremendous one, ranging from the Aristotelian analysis of *vertu* down to such questions of genteel superstition as to whether it is unfair for a duelist to wear an amulet. The theoretical and conceptual side of courtliness is carefully reviewed, not forgetting the somewhat elastic dividing line between nobility of birth and nobility of soul, which has such crucial importance for an understanding of Renaissance art and literature, influenced as they were by the preoccupation of Aristotle and Longinus with the ὕψος . "The French found it easier to measure a gentleman by his inherited position and his family than by trying to decide what qualities he should have inside him." True nobility had to be attested by coats-of-arms authenticated for four generations. And yet even if a gentleman could boast of more than Candide's threescore-and-eleven quarters, there were besides certain formal devotions of the cult to be observed. In the bellicose sixteenth century gentlemen had to "provide leadership and inspiration for victory in the field," even against such unsportsmanlike inventions as artillery. In wartime one had to observe amenities, and the Duc de Nemours could take a cordial morning stroll with Spanish officers shortly before being killed by their men in battle. If one captured a particularly valiant enemy, one should free him, as Lodovico Sforza released Bayard. Gentlemen had to joust, train falcons, hunt the stag and boar, dance, play at *paume*, and divert the ladies, never being bested in these by a person of lower sta-

3. W. L. Wiley, *The Gentleman in Renaissance France* (Cambridge, Mass., 1954).

gentleman must have had a sinking feeling on hearing that the ubiquitous Francis I, with a retinue of 18,000 men and 12,000 horses, was headed his way. (Cellini's estimate.)

Like the *honnête homme*, the *gentilhomme* tended to steer a middle course on social and intellectual issues. Women should be allowed a bit more freedom, but the double standard was still best. As for the religious wars, "it was much easier and more natural for a gentleman to be a Catholic than a Protestant during the Renaissance." Ronsard's "Remonstrance au peuple de France" was a jolly good answer to that noisy voice of Luther "denouncing the polished and cultivated gentleman who loved the arts and polite entertainment, the patron of Raphael and the builder of St. Peter's in Rome." Everyone knew that Italy was a more civilized place than Germany, where the peasants, by the way, seemed to be getting out of hand. The owning and reading of books was desirable, of course, but our French gentleman "was more at ease outdoors with a horse and indoors with a woman than with a book in either place." The new revival of learning was very fine, and one should encourage it even financially, but people must not start rejecting such proved sciences as astrology. Had not Nostradamus prognosticated the death of Henri II seven years ahead of the sad event? All this literary turmoil and writing of sonnets to win an obdurate lady was all right, but any enlightened man of the world knew that a more successful way was to have her served the genitals of a cockerel at supper.

It becomes apparent that Wiley develops lengthily the practices of *cortegiania* in France, as well as extracting its principles. One area of underlying theory neglected by Wiley deserves comment here.

The Renaissance vogue of emblems and devices was a sustaining force to the gentlemanly mode of life. In the first place, many of the devices and plates owed their origins to cavalier heraldry. Giovanni Ferro explained in his *Teatro d'Imprese* that the device was a by-product of knighthood, which was taken over by the academies to be brought to perfection by the men of letters.[4] Henri Estienne quoted Ammirato to the effect that "as some define Poetry to be a Philosophy of Philosophers: that is to say, a delightful meditation of the learned: so we may call a Devise the Philosophie of Cavaliers."[5] And in his *Philosophie des images*, Menestrier made it amply clear that devices and emblems

---

4. Giovanni Ferro, *Teatro d'Imprese* (Venice, 1623), p. 42.
5. Henri Estiennt, *The Art of making Devises* (London, 1646), u. 10.

must be cultivated by the *cortegiano:* he associated emblems with "personnes de qualité," "personnes de premier ordre," "personnes d'esprit," including the king himself. In the *Compleat Gentleman* Henry Peacham advised the courtier to adorn his conversation "with conceits of wit and pleasant invention, as ingenious Epigrams, Emblemes, Anagrams, marrie tales, wittie questions and answers." To the Elizabethan, emblem writing was an essential part of the training of the courtier: "a gentlemanly accomplishment of the same type as the ability to play the lute or dance the lavolta."[6]

The immediate affinities between courtliness and the iconographical movement in literature are attested in divers ways by examination of individual emblem books. Chivalrous virtue, particularly courage and *pundonor* of an ideal knight, was "mirroured" in the *Espejo de principes y cavalleros* of Diego Ortuñez de Calahorra (Zaragoza, 1562). Civic and ethical virtues were emphasized in Bartolommeo del Bene's *Civitas Veri sive Morum* (1609), with its thirty-three copper plates. Roberto Rusca's lecture to the Academy Il Risorgente of Parma appeared as an emblem book, *De Nobilitate,* in 1603. The life of the country gentleman (to which Wiley devotes an informative chapter) was extolled in the emblem book, *Les Plaisirs du gentilhomme champestre* (1581), by Nicolas Rapin of Poitou. An unusual utility is evidenced in Giuliano Bezzi's *Il Torneo, overo Imprese* (1645), which contains devices and rhymes for knights to "carry in the Giostra." It might be added to this sportive justification of emblems that at least two or three emblem books were issued to commemorate *courses de teste et de bague,* as described by Charles Perrault. The chivalrous note behind emblemata is suggested incidentally, by the repeated presence of the adjective "heroic" in the titles. There were scores of heroic devices, emblems, and impresas in both the sixteenth and seventeenth centuries.

Certainly Torquato Tasso's sojourns at typical Renaissance courts in Ferrara, Torino, and elsewhere were responsible for the interest in emblems which led him to write his *Dialogo dell'-Imprese* (Naples, 1594). Indeed, most of the theorists on emblems were familiars at court.

By the seventeenth century, every country of Western Europe had emblem books serving as almanacs or registers of the coats of arms of its greatest nobles. Indeed, in such collections as Jost Amman's *Stammbücher,* coats of arms were interspersed with

6. Rosemary Freeman, *English Emblem Books* (London, 1948), p. 3.

allegories and emblems, an admixture also found in Henry Good-
yer's *The Mirrour of Maiestie, or the Badges of Houour con-
ceitedly emblasoned: with Emblemes* (1618). From Holland,
France, England, and Germany respectively came Alselme de
Boot's *Symbola Varia Diversorum Principum, Archiducum, Do-
cum, Comitum, & Marchionum totius cum facile Isagoge* (1681),
Fineus de Brianville's *Devises héroiques sur les armes de Mon-
seigneur Colbert* (1667), the *Symbola Heroica, or Mottoes of
the Nobility and Baronets of Great Britain* (1736), and the anony-
mous *Schau-Platz Bayerischer Helden* (1681), with its portraits
of sixty-one dukes and their devices.

The Renaissance was a period addicted, long before the notorious contrasts of Baroque, to setting up theses and antitheses
and protagonists and antagonists. There was the *cortegiano* and
the anti-courtier (Falstaff). There was the courtly emblem book
we have been discussing, but similarly, in the vein of Quevedo,
there was an anti-courtier emblem book, the *Emblesmes sus les
actions, perfections, et mœurs du Segnor Espagnol. Traduit de
Castilien* (Mildelbourg, 1605), so popular among the skeptics
and burghers as to be reproduced as *Les Rodomontades et Emblemes Espagnolles* (Rouen, 1637).

Further relationships between emblems and *cortegiania* emerge
in unpredictable ways. The greatest princes of the blood found
themselves and their courtly virtues heralded in emblemata. A
list of rulers of the sixteenth and seventeenth centuries who were
the exalted subjects of emblem books would include the following (names of the emblematists are added parenthetically):
Maximilian (Khuen, Stengel), John of Austria (Sambucus),
Ferdinand IV (Marx), George of Essen (Iselburg), Felipe IV
(Rodríguez de Monforte), Charles II (Ogilby), and Louis XIV
(Le Jay, Le Vavasseur, Menestrier).[7] Menestrier, in fact, seems
to have devoted most of his life to the glorification of the Sun
King. The last triumphs of the *Triumphos morales* (1581) of

7. These emblem books are respectively: Joseph Khuen, *Magnus in ortu,
maximus in meridie*, etc.; Georg Stengel, *Gloria bellica Serenissimi et Poten-
tissimi Principis Maximiliani*, etc.; Joannes Sambucus, *Arcus aliquot triumphai*;
Joannes Marx, *Doron Basilikon*; Peter Iselburg, *Emblematische Gluckwün-
schung*; Pedro Rodríguez de Monforte, *Descripción de las honras*, etc.; John
Ogilby, *Entertainment of his Most Excellent Majestie Charles II*; Gabriel
François Le Jay, *Le Triomphe de la religion sous Louis le Grand*; Pierre Le
Vavasseur, *Ludovico Magno, Symbola heroica*; Claude François Menestrier,
Histoire du roy Louis le Grand par les médailles, emblèmes, devises, etc., and
other works, including his controversial *La Devise du Roy justifiée*.

Francisco de Gómez deal with the exploits of Carlos V and Felipe II in Flanders. This was the age, after all, of the revival of the Pindarism which celebrated kings and heroes. The greatest paragons of *cortegiania* were also the subjects of emblemata, ever since the pioneer emblematist Alciati, as we have reported, made Cadmus the pioneer gentleman. In innumerable cases it was the death of a courtier, such as Francesco Medici, which called forth an emblem book extolling his virtues. The living, too, had their share. There was, for example, Ferrante, Marquis of Pescara, whose forces dealt the chivalrous Bayard a mortal blow. Indeed, Wiley singles him out as a model gentleman, recalling Ferrante's generous statement that he "would give up a 'half gallon of my blood' and not eat meat for two years in order to have Bayard in good health and 'my prisoner.' " Paolo Giovio's emblem "Aut cum hoc, aut in hoc" pictures a shield right out of Vulcan's forge, illustrating how the courtly virtue of the Marquis of Pescara made him set honor above death.

> Lo scudo, di che il figlio, al suo partire
> Di Sparta, orno la generosa madre,
> Dimostra all'huom, che fra l'armate squadre
> Il buon guerrier dee vincere, o morire.[8]

Even if Giovio was aware that Ferrante was the model *cortegiano* to his generation and a "Hector and Achilles of great virtue" to his wife, that brilliant courtly lady was in a sense a paragon and even a custodian of *cortegiania* during her lifetime. Castiglione sent her the manuscript of the *Book of the Courtier* for criticism before it was published. Indeed, as Francisco de Hollanda has shown, she even made the surly and anti-social Michelangelo more gentlemanly by her mere presence. Buonarroti referred in a sonnet to her "immensa cortesia," and Annibal Caro to her "chiara antica nobilitate." Giovio commemorates her stolid qualities by an emblem showing waves beating with vain fury against enduring rocks—the courtly virtue of the Marchioness of Pescara resisting anything unworthy or ignoble. Under the posie, *Conantia frangere frangunt*, Giovio appends the verses:

> Come scoglio percosso in mezzo l'onde,
> Che l'onde istesse da sè batte & spezza,
> Cosi salda virtù discaccia & sprezza
> Tutte opre & voglie illecite & immonde.[9]

8. *Le sententiose imprese di Messer Paolo Giovio et del Sig. Gabriel Symeoni* (Lyon, 1562) p. 86.
9. *Ibid.*, p. 118.

Indeed, some of the emblem books of the Renaissance were written with the intent of the opening lines of the *Orlando Furioso:* to sing of *i cavallieri* and *le cortesie.*

Incidentally, Castiglione, Della Casa, Elyot, Lyly, and Ascham were not the only Renaissance authors busy writing tracts to form the perfect courtier. The emblematists were also occupied in this endeavor. Berlingiero Gessi's *Spada di honore* is a "first book of chivalrous observations." Three of the most popular courtesy books of the time were the *Miroir politicque* of Guillaume de la Perrière (author of the emblematic *Théâtre des bons engins*), *The Compleat Gentleman* of Henry Peacham (author of the emblematic *Minerva Britanna*), and *Civil conversazione* of Guazzo (author of the dialogue on *imprese*). The volume of Gessi is actually an emblem book, containing nine copper plates.

If the emblematists used their books to hail the courtly virtues of great men and their didacticism led some of them to bend their efforts to writing courtesy books, it is not surprising to find how many emblem books were written to instil courtly virtues in the young, *ad usum delphini.* Works of such didactic purpose were the Jesuit Andrés Mendo's *Príncipe perfecto,* Saavedra Faxardo's *Idea de un Príncipe político christiano,* and Ambrogio Marliani's *Theatrum politicum in quo quid agendum sit a Principe.* There were, among others, the Augustinian Barenger's *Guide fidèle à la vraie gloire,* written for the instruction of the young Duke of Burgundy, and Giulio Cesare Capaccio's *Principe,* composed not for any young Borgia but for "any lord whatsoever" ("qualunque Signore"). We remember that Henry Peacham presented manuscripts of emblem books to King James and Prince Henry on the theme "*Basilikon Dorion,* his Majesties Instructions to his dearest Sonne Henrie the Prince." These preceptors of princes, being literary men, generally directed their charges, as did Boissard,[10] toward letters and philosophy, just as Aristotle had directed Prince Alexander. Cesare Ripa congratulated Guarnello for seeking to draw out (educate) the minds of princes with poetry.[11]

Being so rich in metaphor, emblem literature contributed to the maintenance of ceremonies, pageantry, games, and traditions of the court and state. Ripa sets as an aim of his *Nova Iconologia:* "per divisare qualsivoglia apparato Nuttiale, Funerale, Trionfale," an aim shared by the emblem books of Lerch, Strunck,

10. J. J. Boissard, *Icones virorum illustrium,* II, 10.
11. Cesare Ripa, *Iconologia* (Milan, 1602), p. 216.

and others. Praz's bibliography contains an appendix listing such "emblems and devices for festivities, funerals, degrees, etc."[12] Emblems and devices were selected from these and more conventional emblem books by kings and princes to commemorate themselves, even though Henri Estienne was writing that medals served this purpose better than devices. Well known is the salamander of François I, with the motto "Nutrisco et extinguo," reported by both Estienne and Paradin. Louis XII's emblem of the porcupine shocked Tesauro, who objected in his *Cannocchiale Aristotelico* that a "porc espic" was, after all, a "porc." Several scholars have called attention to the passage in Marlowe's *Edward II* where the lords describe to the monarch their device for his triumphal pageant. As a final illustration of the extended utility to courtly virtue of this symbolism which informed emblem literature, there is the emblematic portrait in Chapman's *Byron's Conspiracy*, where Duke Byron and his horse Pastrana are pictured as symbols of royalty ruling and loyalty serving (II, ii, 77-81).

In view of such service in the field of *cortegiania* it was natural that kings and nobles should encourage emblem writers. By 1623 Tesauro could state that the device had reached its highest point, having been taken up by the academies and "now loved and protected by the authority of the greatest princes."[13] Emblemata were prominent in the libraries of Renaissance rulers, and some of these rulers learned of the art directly from the emblematists themselves, as James VI of Scotland learned from Théodore de Bèze.[14] Praz tells how Peter the Great had published in Amsterdam a great volume of *Symbola et emblemata* as "a means of introducing his subjects and ex-boyards to the amenities of western civilization."[15] But by now it was the eleventh hour for both the emblem movement and the Renaissance ideal of *cortegiania*, whose rise and decline coincided in European history.[16]

12. Mario Praz, *Studies in Seventeenth Century Imagery* (London, 1947), II, 180-201.

13. Mario Praz, *Studies in Seventeenth Century Imagery* (London, 1939), I, 64.

14. Henry Green, *Shakespeare and the Emblem Writers* (London, 1870), p. 122.

15. Mario Praz, *op. cit.*, I, 122.

16. For further intelligence on royalty and emblems, see the author's "Princes and Literature: A Theme of Renaissance Emblem Books," *Modern Language Quarterly*, XVI (1955) 114-23.

APPENDIX

BURTON, THE SCALIGERS, AND THE *ANATOMY OF MELANCHOLY*, III, i, 2

NOTES 9 and 16 in the fourth essay of the present volume refer to a passage in the third "partition" of the *Anatomy of Melancholy* illustrating how literary friendships may quickly develop into antagonisms:

Praise and dispraise of each other do as much, though unknown, as Scioppius by Scaliger and Casaubonus: *mulus mulum scabit;* who but Scaliger with him? what encomiums, Epithets, Elogiums! *Antistes sapientiae, perpetuus Dictator, literarum ornamentum, Europae miraculum,* noble Scaliger, *incredibilis ingenii praestantia,* &c. . . . but when they begin to vary, none so absurd as Scaliger, so vile and base, as his books *de Burdone familiā,* and other satirical invectives may witness. Ovid in (his) *Ibis,* Archilochus himself was not so bitter.[1]

It is commonly agreed that Burton is referring in this somewhat cryptic passage to Joseph Justus Scaliger, the learned professor at Leyden. Indeed, the Latin praise quoted above corresponds closely to glowing terms addressed by Scioppius to Joseph Scaliger in a preface (*De arte critica,* Noribergae, 1597), as my friend Vernon Hall reminds me. After the quarrel between Scioppius and Joseph Justus, the former did indeed change his tune. However, in the fourth essay we have permitted the assumption that Burton coupled in his remark Joseph and his famous father Julius-Caesar Scaliger, also called "dictator," a more conspicuous example of the extravagant dispenser of praise and dispraise.[2] The latter's feuds with Erasmus, Rabelais, Dolet, and Cardan were the delight of a century inured to invective as a literary convention. Of his fellow-doctor, Rabelais, he could write the scathing verses we have already translated partially:

> Hic domita ossa piis Baryaeni sunt sita flammis.
> Tetrum non potuit diluere unda nefas.
> Omnia dente canis rosit, solus Deus extra est.
> Cur? quoniam nullum noverat ille Deum.[3]

1. Robert Burton, *The Anatomy of Melancholy,* edited by A. R. Shilleto (London, 1896), III, 24; in the American edition of Floyd Dell and Paul Jordan-Smith (New York, 1938), pp. 628-29.
2. See Paul Jordan-Smith, *Bibliographia Burtoniana* (Stanford University, 1931), pp. 24-25 on Burton's knowledge of both Scaligers, father and son.
3. Julius-Caesar Scaliger, *Poemata* (Geneva, 1591), I, 194.

And of Etienne Dolet:

> Doletus est Terentianus Eunuchus.
> Vult multa multum: pauca sed parum praestat.
> Tamen tonabit, fulguransque clamabit,
> Horum farina aspersus esse pistrini.[4]

Julius-Caesar Scaliger became known as "le tondeur" because of his attacks on contemporaries, attacks which led Erasmus to observe that he sought out antagonists.[5]

There are several reminiscences of the elder Scaliger in Burton's passage. Although the father's assaults were contained in letters, pamphlets, and poetry, the greatest paroxysm of scurrilous epigrammata can be found in that section of his *Poemata* entitled "Archilochus," the archetype who, in Burton's words, "was not so bitter." Burton may well have remembered that in another section entitled "Heroes," Julius-Caesar Scaliger emulated the wrathful invective of the *Ibis*, written during Ovid's exile, by penning a malediction, "P. Ovidius Naso," supposedly sent to Augustus in Rome and beginning

> A me utinam inciperes ferus esse cruente: nec atras
> Per caedes faceres ad mea fata gradum
> Si mea te movit tetricum lasciva iuventus,
> Te iuvenem damnas perditus: exul abi. . . .[6]

Yet at the same time Julius-Caesar Scaliger could illustrate Burton's point about flattery and adulation. He "began to vary," as we have seen, by revising his criticisms of Erasmus. His affection for George Buchanan, Étienne de la Boétie, Matteo Bandello, and others drove him to encomiums, epithets, and elogiums as unbridled as his condemnations.[7] These praises, as Burton suggests ("who but Scaliger with him?") were reciprocated.[8] *Mulus mulum scabit.*

Joseph Justus Scaliger was on the other hand a man of more mild and well-disposed temperament, as all evidence shows,

---

4. *Ibid.*, I, 429.

5. Preserved Smith, *Erasmus* (New York, 1923), p. 314.

6. Julius-Caesar Scaliger, *Poemata, ed. cit.*, I, 328.

7. Typical salutes to Buchanan, La Boétie, and Bandello are found in Julius-Caesar Scaliger's *Poemata, ed. cit.*, I, 178, 345; I, 20-21, 420, 423-24; I, 327. He also dedicated his *Heroinae* to Bandello.

8. For "reciprocal scratching" see George Buchanan, *Poémata* (Leyden, 1628), p. 336; Etienne de la Boétie, *Œuvres complètes* (Bordeaux, 1892), pp. 223-24; 243-44; Matteo Bandello, *Tutte le opere* (Milan, 1934-35), II, 847, 944, 1085, 1199, 1200.

including a reading of his letters.[9] He enters the picture as the pious inheritor of his father's feuds and fondnesses, the second-generation executor who must slowly clean up accounts. Thus, when Schoppe (Scioppius) dispraises his father or Casaubon praises him, it is the son who must now handle the responses. Let us look briefly at the situations with Schoppe and Casaubon, who, incidentally, indulged in their own feud after Schoppe attacked Casaubon's anti-Jesuitical *Epistola ad Frontonem*.

Even long after his death, the epistolary and poetic vituperations of Julius-Caesar Scaliger left rancor among the humanists of the succeeding generation, including Burton himself, as we shall see. So it was that Gaspard Schoppe attacked his claim to being a descendant of the princely Veronese family of the Della Scala, a claim that Julius had often made and which Joseph reported in his *Epistola de vetustate et splendore gentis Scaligerae et Julii Caesaris Scaligeri vita* (1594).[10] Schoppe charged in his *Scaliger Hypobolimaeus* (1607) that Julius was the son of a sign-painter, Benedetto Bordoni, and when the son riposted with a *Confutatio stultissimae Burdonum fabulae auctore* (1608), one of the titles simplified by Burton to *De Burdonum familia*, the quarrel gained renewed momentum.[11]

The same bridging of generations is found in the case of Isaac Casaubon (1559-1614). This Hellenist declared that Julius-Caesar's writings were equal to those of Aristotle.[12] Burton's miscellany of Latin epithets to Joseph Justus, reproduced above, parallels not only Casaubon's praises, but the outpouring of adulation which lasted from Julius's death in 1558 to the period in which the *Anatomy* was published. Son Joseph Justus responded to the "scratching" of Casaubon. In his *Schedia encomiastica seu encomia librorum* he finds Casaubon's edition of

9. George W. Robinson, *Autobiography of Joseph Scaliger* (Cambridge, Mass., 1927), pp. 37-55. Contains letters written from Leyden. Other less available editions are *Epistolae nunc primum collectae ac editae* (Leyden, 1627) and *Lettres françaises de Joseph Scaliger* (Agen, 1879), edited by Tamizey de Larroque.

10. Joseph Scaliger, *Epistola de vetustate et splendore gentis Scaligerae* (Leyden, 1594). The reissue of 1627 would indicate that Joseph Justus had the last word.

11. The feuds with Schoppe, Rabelais, Erasmus, and Cardan are precisely summarized in Vernon Hall, *Life of Julius-Caesar Scaliger* (Philadelphia, 1950), pp. 87, 93; 99-105; 110-14; 91-92; 114-16, 146-48; 140-46.

12. Charles Nisard, *Les gladiateurs de la république des lettres* (Paris, 1860), I, 381.

Suetonius a "Caesarian" accomplishment.[13] He dedicates his *Florilegium epigrammatum Martialis* "ad clarissimum et eximiae eruditionis virum Isaacum Casaubonum," appending dedicatory verses in Greek and Latin.[14] On his side, Casaubon's praise extended to the second generation of Scaligers as well. In 1604 he writes from Madrid to congratulate Petrus Sciverius on publishing Joseph's *Poemata graeca versa*, "tantus elegantiarum thesaurus," and has no scruples about comparing them advantageously with the models by Aristophanes, Euripides, and Sophocles.[15]

But it is upon the key proverb "mule scratcheth mule" that we rest our contention that it was Julius as well as Joseph whom Burton compounded in his archetype of mutable critic. This proverb has troubled the editors of Burton. A. R. Shilleto thought it an evocation of Ausonius, idyll xii ("Claw me, and I'll claw thee!").[16] Floyd Dell and Paul Jordan-Smith thought that Burton was repeating Scioppius' pun on the name Bordone (Lat. *burdonis*, "from a mule").[17] Yet Burton makes no apparent effort here to point up a pun; he merely simplifies the long-winded Latin titles of Joseph's biography of his father and his subsequent refutation.

The source of Burton's key proverb is not Ausonius or Scioppius. It is Julius-Caesar Scaliger himself. In two of his "apicular" pieces, "In mutuos laudatores" and "De mutuis laudatoribus," Julius gets to thinking about the literary feuds, alignments, and coteries of his time, as Burton was to do. The first poem is contained in that section of the *Poemata* entitled "Hipponax," after the bitter Greek satirist:

> Suos amicos quisque cum canit vates,
> Se mutuas captare sat docet laudes.
> Sic foeneratur ille nomen, & famam.
> Verbum vetus fit: *Mutuum scabunt muli.*[18]

The second occurrence of the proverb is in that section with the equally appropriate rubric of "Archilochus":

> Multis benigne versibus bonos malis
> Appellat, & salutat, & gestit leuis,
> Pares Baraenus indidem expectans vices.

13. Joseph Justus Scaliger, *Poemata omnia* (Leyden, 1615), p. 53.
14. Joseph Justus Scaliger, *Poemata graeca versa* (Leyden, 1615), pp. 1, 3.
15. *Ibid.*, p. v.
16. Shilleto edition, III, 24.
17. Dell and Jordan-Smith edition, p. 1035.
18. Julius-Caesar Scaliger, *Poemata, ed. cit.*, I, 441.

Contra benigne pauculi paucis eum
Raro salutant gestientem versibus,
Operas Baraeno sic reponentes pares.
Hoc est, quod aiunt: *Mutuum muli scabunt.*
   Fictis amici et nomine, & versu, & modo
Blande teipsum ac turgide appellas vafer,
Baraene titillator astutus tui.
   am hos est *teipsum mulus, haud muli scabunt.*[19]

Aware of these elaborations of his key proverb and, indeed, remembering this latter exploitation of it against poor Rabelais (Baraenus), viewed as an eager flatterer ill repaid, Burton is moved to irony. Whereas he himself could poke amiable fun at Rabelais—he saw François as an appropriate medic for the inmates of Bedlam[20]—he deems "vile and base" the constant and finally humorless vituperation against Rabelais (as Bibinus, Baraenus, Baryoenus, *etc.*) throughout the *Poemata*. This unceasing stream of "iambics" against Rabelais turned Burton against Julius-Caesar Scaliger, just as it eventually soured even such admirers of Scaliger as Jean Voulté (Vulteius).[21] Despite Burton's great respect for the learning and authority of Julius-Caesar Scaliger, whom he occasionally quoted in the *Anatomy* as arbiter on social and philosophical matters, he is struck by the hypocrisy of Scaliger as a participant in mutual flattery and hyperbole (*e.g.*, the section "Heroes" of the *Poemata*) who accuses others of indulging in them. Thus we feel that the irony of the *mulus mulum scabit* passage is directed at the "old campaigner" Julius-Caesar Scaliger as much as at Gaspard Schoppe, antagonist of both generations of Scaligers.

19. *Ibid.*, I, 354.
20. Shilleto edition, I, 137. On Rabelais, see also I, 262, 391; III, 440.
21. Jean Voulté, *Epigrammata* (Lyon, 1537), p. 172. Quoted in Vernon Hall, *op. cit.*, p. 115.

INDEX

The Department of Romance Studies Digital Arts and Collaboration Lab at the University of North Carolina at Chapel Hill is proud to support the digitization of the North Carolina Studies in the Romance Languages and Literatures series.

DEPARTMENT OF
Romance Studies
Digital Arts and Collaboration Lab

www.ingramcontent.com/pod-product-compliance
Lightning Source LLC
Chambersburg PA
CBHW021233020726
47498CB00008B/2824

* 9 7 8 0 8 0 7 8 9 0 3 1 8 *